Informal Logic Examples and Exercises

Informal Logic Examples and Exercises

Malcolm Acock

Wadsworth Publishing Company
Belmont, California
A Division of Wadsworth, Inc.

Philosophy Editor: Kenneth King
Production Editor: Jane Townsend
Managing Designer: Cynthia Bassett
Designer: Edith Allgood
Copy Editor: Elaine Linden
Cover: Cheryl Carrington
Print Buyer: Barbara Britton

Printed in the United States of America
1 2 3 4 5 6 7 8 9 10—89 88 87 86 85

ISBN 0-534-04494-8

Library of Congress Cataloging in Publication Data

Acock, Malcolm.
   Informal logic examples and exercises.

   1. Logic—Problems, exercises, etc. I. Title.
BC108.A26 1985   160′.76   84–20810
ISBN 0-534-04494-8

Contents

To the Instructor

In teaching a course in informal logic, I have found that my greatest aid is a large stock of "real" examples. Abstractions can be formulated and stated in class, but their application to examples and the discussion of examples is important to students' understanding. Further examples are required for out-of-class practice by students, for homework assignments, and for use on tests and examinations. Most texts don't contain a sufficient number of examples to satisfy all these needs, and any instructor who teaches an informal logic course regularly gets bored with repeatedly discussing the same examples.

It is beneficial for the examples to be "real"—that is, culled from everyday sources and from disciplines outside of philosophy—rather than made up by a textbook author. Made-up examples are usually tedious and boring for both student and instructor; real examples can be interesting and entertaining. Real examples demonstrate to students that the study of informal logic is useful and applies both to their everyday life and to whatever academic discipline they are pursuing. Many texts on informal logic contain only made-up examples—and any course that uses such a text alone suffers accordingly.

Since the time I began teaching a course in informal logic, I have slowly accumulated a stock of real examples. This collection of examples has continued to grow and to be useful no matter what text I have used in the course (and I have used several different ones).

This book is, primarily, a collection of exercises composed of real examples. The book is divided into sixteen sections, each of which considers a different topic. These topics will not necessarily correlate one-for-one with class periods; some topics may demand more than one class (for example, the two sections on deductive logic), whereas others may not require a whole class period.

My selection of topics is, of course, not that of every textbook author. However, the topics addressed in this book cover what I consider to be the central issues in informal logic. The majority of texts cover most of the topics discussed in the various sections of this book. It is possible, of course, to omit some of the topics I include or to include topics I omit.

Likewise, the order in which I take up topics indicates my preference, which might not be shared universally. Basically, the topics covered fall into four categories:

1. Features of language—quotation marks, meaning, ambiguity, connotation, and the like—discussion of which I consider to be a necessary preliminary to the identification and analysis of arguments.
2. General analysis of arguments: recognizing the component parts of arguments and diagraming and evaluating them.
3. Deductively valid (maximally good) propositional logic and quantificational logic.
4. Fallacious arguments.

However, the examples from the various sections of this book can be used whether or not this order of presentation is followed.

Although this book is intended as a collection of exercises to *supplement* a text in informal logic, each group of exercises is preceded by a short introduction and brief instructions. The introduction gives a highly condensed outline of the topic illustrated by several examples. Many of these introductions of necessity avoid or gloss over difficulties and complexities in the topic. A text that goes into such details or very full discussion of such issues in class is essential to amplify these brief outlines.

The instructions specify what is to be done to the examples in the exercise sections. In the instructions for the exercises on argument analysis, I have used diagraming techniques that I find powerful and that I believe are gaining widespread acceptance in the discipline. However, these techniques are not used universally in texts on informal logic. If the techniques I use are not those of the text you use, either the diagraming techniques can be introduced to complement the techniques in the text or the student can be advised to ignore the relevant introductions and instructions. The examples in this book should be of use no matter what text is used.

Sufficient examples are included to allow some examples to be discussed when the topic is originally introduced in class, some to be used for homework assignments, some for additional practice by students, and some to be used on tests. Obviously, there are some examples that are more suited to class discussion than others. I have found that if students know that some test questions might be taken from examples they have been given but have not been required to work, they are encouraged to practice with the supplementary examples.

The book is designed so that, where appropriate, printed passages can be marked up and analyses given on the same page before the page is torn from the book and handed in as a homework assignment. This feature has two main purposes: It saves the students having to write out the passage before they analyze it, allowing more examples to be assigned for homework, and it eases grading because the passage being marked up is uniform from one student's homework to the next and legible (which is not always the case when students have to copy the passage). By having students mark up the printed passage and tear out the pages, everybody's burden is eased. The burden on the instructor is further eased if students can be persuaded to mark up the passage in an ink color distinct from both the black print and the color of the grader's pen.

I have found that writing examples on transparencies and then displaying them in class with the use of an overhead projector enormously improves the efficiency of each class. Students will have the passage being discussed before them in the book—they become bored if they have to wait while the instructor writes the example on the blackboard. Moreover, once it is on an overhead transparency you never have to write it out again and you can avoid the mess of chalk. More examples can be discussed in class if no one has to take time to write out the example. So committing these examples— particularly those that require the marking up of the passage—to transparencies is beneficial to everyone and allows for a more productive use of class time.

In the introduction to each section there are references to texts that give more comprehensive discussions of the topic or topics of that section. Also, inside the front cover there is a table showing how the sections of this book correlate with some leading texts on informal logic.

I would like to thank Paul Roth, University of Missouri, St. Louis, who reviewed the manuscript, and Cathy Hardin, who typed it. Also, I encourage you to communicate to me your criticisms of, and comments on, this book and to share with me examples you find particularly interesting.

To the Student

This book is primarily a book of exercises covering the sorts of things that are discussed in courses on informal logic. The exercises are composed of "real" examples—that is, they have not been made up for such courses. In choosing the examples, I have attempted to show that the content of a course in informal logic is relevant both to your everyday life and to whatever academic discipline is your major interest. A lot of examples come from everyday sources—newspapers, newsmagazines, even some radio and television programs. Other examples come from novels, books on astronomy, backpacking, economics, and so on in an effort to illustrate that understanding arguments is important in any discipline or interest.

To some extent, of course, the items reflect what I read, where I happen to be living currently, and what my major interests are. However, I have made a conscious effort to find some examples from sources outside what I normally read. Some items included here were first brought to my attention by friends and students. I have systematically excluded examples from my major field of interest—philosophy—but even so, some of my other interests—for example, computer science and artificial intelligence—will probably be obvious from the examples.

At the beginning of each set of exercises there is a short introduction explaining the topic or topics that the examples illustrate and a brief set of instructions about what is to be done to the examples. The short introduction is not a substitute for a more extended discussion of the topic, which can be found in a regular text. If the text you are using doesn't discuss a particular topic, consult the references listed in the introduction.

In the instructions in each section, I have used the techniques of analysis that I favor. Not all books in informal logic use the same techniques; thus in working the exercises you should follow the procedures specified by your instructor. However, the techniques I use are easy to learn and *complement* different techniques of analysis. Whatever techniques your instructor employs, the examples may be analyzed using those techniques.

The analysis of some of the examples involves "marking up" the printed passage. The pages of the book are perforated so that, where appropriate, the printed page can be written on and then torn out of the book and handed in as a homework assignment. For marking up passages, I suggest that you use a color of ink other than black (the color of the print) and other than the color used by your instructor for grading (red?); this way, when homework is returned it will be easy to see what is in the original passage, how you marked it up, and what changes your instructor made.

At the end of the book there are several worked examples from each section. These are kept to a minimum to allow space for as many examples as possible with which to practice. However, enough worked examples are given to further illustrate the techniques specified in the instructions in each section. Worked examples are marked with an asterisk (*) where they occur in the text. For maximum benefit, try working these examples *before* you turn to the end of the book and see how they are worked there.

I hope the examples in the book show you how widely applicable and how useful informal logic is. I also hope you find some of the examples interesting and some amusing. Finally, if you have comments (positive or negative), or examples you discover that you particularly like, I hope you will share them with me.

Section 1

Quotation Marks: Direct Quotes, Scare Quotes, Use/Mention Quotes

Introduction

The topic of the examples in this first section is the use of quotation marks. There are three main uses of quotation marks: to indicate direct quotation, to serve as scare quotes, and to observe the use/mention distinction.

Direct Quotes

Quotation marks are sometimes used to indicate that the words enclosed in the quotes are exactly the words that were originally spoken or written. Usually, double quotes are used to indicate direct quotation.

Scare Quotes

Scare quotes indicate that the words enclosed in quotes are being used in an unusual way and that their usual meaning is not the one intended (as with the technical usage of a word from some special discipline such as science, mathematics, or the law). For example:

> *In World War II the Germans made "coffee" from roasted acorns.*

Some authors use double quotes, whereas others use single quotes, as scare quotes.

Use/Mention Quotes

Use/mention quotes are placed around a linguistic item (a word, name, phrase, sentence, and the like) to form a name of that linguistic item whenever we want to talk about the word rather than the thing to which the word refers. For example:

> *'Mick Jagger' has ten letters.*
> *Mick Jagger leads the Rolling Stones.*

Direct quotation marks and scare quotes are commonly used and therefore familiar. However, some authors do not use use/mention quotes at all and others use them inconsistently. Thus, whereas some of the examples in this section concern direct quotation marks and scare quotes, most of them concern the use of use/mention quotes.

It is important to clarify the use of use/mention quotes at the beginning of any study of informal logic because, as we study arguments, we often want to talk about component parts of these arguments such as sentences, phrases, and words. Correct use of use/mention quotes clarifies written passages in which we talk about such linguistic items.

Usually, we observe the use/mention distinction by placing the linguistic item in quotes, either

1. double quotes, as in the first line of exercise 1–8, or
2. single quotes, as in the first line of exercise 1–24. However,
3. some authors italicize words they are mentioning rather than using, as in exercise 1–19, and
4. if we wish to mention a number of words, names, and so on, it is acceptable to simply list them after a colon or a dash at the end of a sentence, as in the last two lines of exercises 1–8 and 1–31. Finally,
5. if one set of use/mention quotes occurs embedded within another set, it is customary to alternate the use of double quotes and single quotes.

Not all books on informal logic discuss the use of quotation marks and the use/mention distinction; however, you will find discussions in the following two books:

Ronald Munson, *The Way of Words,* pp. 11–17

Howard Kahane, *Logic and Philosophy,* 4th ed., pp. 370–371

It might seem unnecessarily picky to insist on the observation of the use/mention distinction, but this is not so. The distinction is of great importance in at least one very practical matter—computer languages. As an example, imagine you have written, in the computer language BASIC, a program that adds together any two numbers and stores the result in a memory location you have named 'SUM'; following which you have supplied as data the two numbers 24 and 40 to be added together. If one line of the program is the instruction

PRINT SUM

this will cause the printer to print as output what 'SUM' refers to — the value

64

However, if a line of the program contains the instruction

PRINT 'SUM'

this will cause the printer to print as output

SUM

This is the use/mention distinction: In the first PRINT statement, the word 'SUM' is *used* to designate what it refers to—that is, the memory location that currently stores the value 64; whereas in the second PRINT statement, the word 'SUM' is *mentioned* (by forming a name for it by putting it in single quotes) as the word that is to be printed. By observing the use/mention distinction, we are able to write the instructions

PRINT 'SUM= '

PRINT SUM

to produce as output

SUM= 64

All computer languages make the use/mention distinction in similar ways.

Section 1: Instructions

In the exercises of Section 1:

1. Check to determine whether the use/mention distinction has been correctly and consistently observed.
2. Where the distinction has not been correctly observed, supply the required quotation marks. For example, if the given passage was

Ale has one less letter than beer

quotes should be added to give

'Ale' has one less letter than 'beer'.

3. Where the distinction has been correctly observed and there are quotes in the passage, state what kind of quotes they are and explain why the author used them. For example, consider the following as the given passage:

Some investigators critical of parapsychological experiments claim that 'ESP' is not an acronym for 'extrasensory perception'—"perception" by some means other than the five senses—but rather for 'error some place'.

For this passage, the required explanations are as follows:

The single quotes around 'ESP', 'extrasensory perception', and 'error some place', are all use/mention quotes. The author used them to make it clear that he is talking about words and phrases occurring inside the quotes, rather than the things to which the words refer. The double quotes around 'perception' are scare quotes. They indicate that here the word 'perception' is being used in an unusual and extended way—normally, 'perception' means perception by one of the five senses.

In the exercises in later sections, continue to be on the lookout for places where authors have not used use/mention quotes but should have. There are further examples in Section 2 and elsewhere.

Section 1: Exercises

1-1 Jim Gillis, a senior philosophy major, and his partner, Bob Poretto, were told Aug. 2 they could not use the word "saloon" in the title of their nightclub . . . a law put on the Alabama books in the 1930s prohibits the use of the words "bar buffet, or saloon" in the name of businesses that serve alcohol . . .

"It's also against the law to use the words "beer, whiskey, wine and ale" on your signs and other places are breaking that law," he [Gillis] said . . . .

"The A.B.C. directive to the Southside Saloon disallows five words from being used in a sign," he [an A.B.C. official] said. "Saloon is one of them and ale isn't." ("Saloon Fighting for the Right to Keep Name," by Charlie Ingram, *Kaleidoscope,* September 30, 1983, p. 2)

*1-2 The [computer] program would note that new radios cost money and that people go to banks to withdraw money, and so it would "reason" that Mary probably went to the bank to get money to buy the radio. ("Artificial Intelligence," by David L. Waltz, *Scientific American,* October 1982, p. 132)

1-3 Whatever the reason, in my private lexicon of gastronomy I continue to see the word exquisite ringed about with the subtle vapors of perversion. ("E Is for Exquisite," in *An Alphabet for Gourmets* in *The Art of Eating,* by M. F. K. Fisher, p. 600)

1-4 Tallulah remained a virgin all through these New York years until she was twenty, a virginal virgin up to the age of seventeen, a "technical virgin" up to the time when she left the country. She made that claim in her autobiography, *Tallulah,* and there is no reason to doubt it. "I use the phrase 'technical virgin' advisedly," she wrote. "I had my share of necking. More than once I trembled on the brink of compliance." (*Miss Tallulah Bankhead,* by Lee Israel, p. 61)

1-5 Says Joyce Copland, director of marketing at Addison-Wesley Publishing Co.: "You could probably print napkins with the word computer on them and sell them like crazy." ("Computers: The New Hardware Made Easy," by Phillip Faflick, *Time,* January 24, 1983, p. 91)

*1-6 You know, and I know, that détente is a word that will last only as long as the balance of power exists. (*The Windchime Legacy,* by A. W. Mykel, p. 80)

1-7 And what about the president's "Task Force on Food Assistance"? " 'Hunger' sounds so down," explains one White House official. . . .

There's also "pro-life" and "pro-choice." Everybody knows that pro-life means anti-abortion, but pro-life sounds so much nicer. Who *isn't* pro-life? Consider the alternative. The pro-abortion people, not eager to use a radioactive word like abortion have

---

*Exercises marked with an asterisk are those included in the *Worked Exercises* section in the back of the book.

jumped right in. What's *their* alternative? "Pro-repression"? ("Newspeak—Washington Version," by Elisabeth Bumiller, *Washington Post* section of *Manchester Guardian Weekly*, September 18, 1983, p. 16. Reprinted by permission)

1-8   Ten years ago the word "algorithm" was unknown to most educated people; indeed, it was scarcely necessary. The rapid rise of computer science, which has the study of algorithms as its focal point, has changed all that; the word is now essential. There are several other words that almost, but not quite, capture the concept that is needed: procedure, recipe, process, routine, method, rigamarole. ("Algorithms," by Donald E. Knuth, *Scientific American*, April 1977, p. 63)

*1-9 "In my opinion the delegates should not be bound to vote for any particular candidate . . . This would be the democratic way—and I am spelling democratic with a small 'd'." (Senator Byrd quoted in *Manchester Guardian Weekly*, August 10, 1980, p. 6)

1-10 Bahia, or San Salvador. Brazil, Feb. 29th.—The day passed delightfully. Delight itself, however, is a weak term to express the feelings of a naturalist who, for the first time, has wandered by himself in a Brazilian forest. (*Voyage of the Beagle*, by Charles Darwin, p. 11)

1-11 On medieval philosophers: "it is not only true that they never discovered the steam engine; it is quite equally true that they never tried."
       Notice, if you will, the balance in the contrasting clauses: "not only true" is balanced against "quite equally true." "Small virtues" carries the same weight as "enormous crimes." Verbs match verbs, adjectives match adjectives. Try your hand, and improve your style. ("Try Your Hand and Improve," *Birmingham News*, June 27, 1982, p. 3F)

1-12 *Flea markets*, too, whether commercially or charitably promoted, will normally accept any entrants. This includes antiques, "junktiques," and just plain junk as well as crafts. Again, you may find a gem of a jeweler among the trash, but . . . ("Meet Me at the Fair," by Elizabeth V. Warren, *House Beautiful*, March 1979, p. 68)

1-13 This section introduces such basic terms as axon, dendrites, synapse, and threshold and may be omitted by any reader who has studied the bare elements of neurophysiology. (*The Metaphorical Brain*, by Michael A. Arbib, p. 18)

1-14 And each [creative scientist] had initially conceived of the hypothesis in an intuitive "flash" (later backed up by documentary evidence). ("Science and the Unconscious," by M.-L. Franz, in *Man and His Symbols*, ed. Carl G. Jung et al., pp. 379–380)

1-15 The world sprang into being five minutes ago, exactly as it then was, with a population that "remembered" a wholly unreal past. (*The Analysis of Mind*, by Bertrand Russell, pp. 157–160)

1-16 A printer with proportional spacing produces characters that occupy no more space than their width requires. (The letter i, for example, takes less space than w.) ("Computers, Part 2—How to Choose a Printer," *Consumer Reports*, October 1983, p. 532)

1-17 "Tutankhamen is . . . the name of a mysterious boy king who died, aged 18 or 19, and was buried in a hidden tomb near Luxor 3,200 years ago." ("Unsolved Riddle of the Sands," by Hugh Herbert, *Manchester Guardian Weekly*, March 4, 1979, p. 20)

1-18 No such reluctance encumbers that American word-master, Willard R. Espy. He revels in ribaldry, notably in the rich fields of the proper and improper noun. Ribald, for instance. From the works of Jean Ribaut who claimed the territory of Florida for the French? Not so, I think. They were as clean as a whistle. The Old High German for whore (Hriba) is probably the origin. And from thence, questionably, came "whore moans." Wince not, gentle reader. Etymology is a Tom Tiddler's ground for speculators. And sex is older than Olduvai; not even the Russians claim to have invented it. ("Good Clean Fun," by John Hillaby, *New Scientist*, April 26, 1979, p. 294. Reprinted by permission)

1-19 He had been thrown off by an ambiguity in the term *quality*. He wondered why that ambiguity should exist, made a mental note to do some digging into the historic roots of the word *quality*, then put it aside. (*Zen and the Art of Motorcycle Maintenance*, by Robert M. Pirsig, pp. 231–232)

1-20 That four-letter word has joined the list of unparliamentary expressions alongside blackguard, blether, and traitor. The Speaker of the House, Mr. George Thomas, told the Commons last week that from now on the word was strictly out of order. He said: "So far as I am concerned as long as I am Speaker I shall consider that an unparliamentary expression." As an unparliamentary expression, it will now be entered in Erskine May, the official bible of Parliament, alongside such words as 'calumny,' 'dishonest,' 'duplicity,' 'guttersnipe' and 'hooligan.' ("Speaker Bans That Word," by Colin Brown, *Manchester Guardian Weekly*, February 14, 1982, p. 4)

1-21 Now the serpent was more subtle than any other wild creature that the Lord God had made. He said to the woman, "Did God say, 'you shall not eat of any tree of the garden'?" And the woman said to the serpent, "We may eat of the fruit of the trees of the garden; but God said, 'You shall not eat of the fruit of the tree which is in the midst of the garden, neither shall you touch it, lest you die.' " (Genesis 3:1–3)

1-22 When the historian says, this happened, that is always an abbreviated phrase for, the available evidence points to this having happened. ("Some Problems of the Philosophy of History," by G. C. Field, *Proceedings of the British Academy*, 1938, p. 70)

1-23   For clarity I shall adopt the following convention: the term macroinstruction will refer to a software instruction and the term microinstruction will refer to a firmware instruction. ("Microprogramming," by David A. Patterson, *Scientific American*, March 1983, p. 50)

1-24   Northport—"It bothers me that so many people think 'utilitarian' is a dirty word," potter Susan V. Brown says. "It is important to me for the pieces I make to be used, not just set on a shelf and admired." ("Don't Set Her Pottery on a Shelf," by Elma Bell, *Birmingham News*, March 1, 1981, p. 1D)

1-25   "Fill" a gasoline or kerosene stove by pouring fuel carefully into the tank until it's only about three quarters full. (*Backpacking*, by Michael Sandi, p. 171)

1-26   We might conjecture that the "natural athlete" has no magical, global coordination faculty but only (or should we say "only!") has worked out for himself an unusually expressive abstract scheme for manipulating representations of physical activities. (*Artificial Intelligence*, by Marvin Minsky and Seymour Papert, p. 46)

1-27   In recent years a good deal of confusion has arisen about the meaning of the term microprogramming, owing largely to the advent of the microprocessor, the "computer on a chip" that is at the heart of the latest products of the progressive miniaturization of silicon-based semiconductor technology. ("Microprogramming," by David A. Petterson, *Scientific American*, March 1983, p. 50)

1-28   As I am writing this: I'm thinking about the word again. I am thinking that it is a relative of the word rain. They have so much in common. ("Autumn Trout Gathering," *Tokyo-Montana Express*, by Richard Brautigan, p. 27)

1-29   Beyond this the main trick of science is to *really* think of something: the shape of the clouds and their occasional sharp bottom edges at the same altitude everywhere in the sky; the formation of a dewdrop on a leaf; the origin of a name or a word—Shakespeare, say, or 'philanthropic'; the reason for human social customs—the incest taboo, for example. ("Can We Know the Universe? Reflections on a Grain of Salt," *Broca's Brain: Reflections on the Romance of Science*, by Carl Sagan, pp. 13–14)

1-30   I had barely recovered from the appellative blow struck by SoHo (*South of Houston* Street) when I received a quick left to the sensibility in the form of NoHo (*North of Houston* Street). Head bloody but unbowed, I dropped my guard and TriBeCa (*Triangle Below Canal* Street) scored a T.K.O. in the very first sound. ("City Limiting: The New Geography," *Metropolitan Life*, by Fran Lebowitz, p. 104)

1-31 Brebeuf Island is named after the Jesuit missionary who was killed there by the Indians.
Penetanguishene is an Indian name, and the townships of Tiny, Tay and Flo were
named after the lap dogs of Lady Sarah Maitland. . . .
Some melancholy names speak for themselves—Mel-de-Mere, Go Home Bay, and Bad
Neighbor Rock. ("A Mosaic of Names," *Canada Today/d'aujourd'hui*, No. 5, 1983,
p. 11)

1-32 The Ebers Papyrus of about 1500 B.C. describes various Egyptian "cures" for diabetes,
though no cure exists even today, only remedies. (*The Big, Fertile, Rumbling, Cast-Iron,
Growling, Aching, Unbuttoned Bellybook,* by James Trager, p. 413)

*1-33 Then it [Havana] became the main port and assembly point for the trans-shipment to
Spain of the vast treasures extracted from the Western hemisphere. Coffee, tobacco
(like hammock and hurricane, an original Carib word), and later sugar added to the
burgeoning wealth of the great city. ("Cuba Battens Down the Hatches," by John Ret-
tie, *Manchester Guardian Weekly,* November 13, 1983, p. 8)

1-34 I am wary of the words pessimism and optimism. ("Afterword: A Talk with the Author," by Milan Kundera, in *The Book of Laughter and Forgetting,* p. 237)

Section 2

Meaning and Definition

Introduction

Definitions and meanings are the subjects of the examples in this section.

It is possible to talk about the meaning of nonlinguistic items. For example, we might say that a brilliantly colorful sunset means there is bad atmospheric pollution. Here 'means' means indicates or signifies. However, ordinarily it is linguistic items—words, phrases, sentences, and so on—that we talk about as having meanings. A definition is, of course, merely a specification of the meaning of some linguistic item.

We might think that an "ideal" definition would specify a set of conditions, where each condition by itself is necessary and the set of conditions taken together is sufficient (so-called "individually necessary and jointly sufficient conditions") for giving the meaning of the term being defined. Sometimes definitions attain this "ideal"—for example, in exact disciplines such as mathematics and the law. In mathematics, 'rectangle' can be defined by two individually necessary and jointly sufficient conditions: (a) a closed, four-sided, two-dimensional figure, (b) having equal internal angles. Each of these conditions is individually necessary because for 'rectangle' to correctly apply to something, that thing must satisfy each of these conditions. They are jointly sufficient because if both of the conditions are satisfied by something, that is enough to establish that 'rectangle' applies to that thing.

However, most definitions fall far short of meeting these two requirements; and indeed, there is reason to think that many words in general use in ordinary language could never be given such precise definitions. Dictionary definitions, for example, usually attempt to give the most obvious features of the things generally referred to by the term being defined. Many definitions don't even attempt this much, but rather merely try to give you a general idea, perhaps by giving examples (what might be called " 'Love is a warm puppy' definitions").

One very important distinction is that between reportive and stipulative definitions. (a) Reportive definitions give an account of how some word is (or was), in fact, used by some linguistic community (group of people speaking the same language or dialect). (b) Stipulative definitions specify how a certain term is to be used in a particular context.

There are various ways in which definitions can fail to be satisfactory. Some of the most important are as follows:

1. A definition is given in terms of necessary and sufficient conditions, but the conditions are not individually necessary and/or are not jointly sufficient. An example is defining 'fossil' as the remains or imprint of an animal that lived in an earlier era. This condition is not necessary, for fossils can be of plants as well as of animals; and it is not sufficient, because the remains of an animal frozen into a sheet of ice in some past age would satisfy the "definition," but would not be a fossil.

2. A definition that is not specific enough to indicate the difference in meaning between the term being defined and some different term. An example is defining 'stool' as a piece of furniture with legs that is used for sitting upon. This "definition" is inadequate in that it is not specific enough to differentiate between 'stool' and 'chair'.

3. A definition is circular; that is, the definition uses the term being defined. For example, if we defined 'igneous rock' as a rock produced by igneous geological processes, someone not knowing the meaning of 'igneous' and/or 'rock' would not be able to understand this definition, and if they knew the meaning of the words they would not need it.

4. A definition is worded in such vague and general terms that it does not allow us to decide when the definition is satisfied. An example is defining 'plane' as a geographical area where there are only small changes in elevation. One problem with this "definition" is the vagueness of 'small'—how large can a change in elevation be and still be considered small: 10, 50, 100, or 1,000 feet?

Definitions can suffer from more than one of these problems at the same time. The fourth example illustrates this because not only is the proposed definition too vague, but also, while it gives a set of sufficient conditions for the use of 'plane', these conditions are not necessary—they are not satisfied, for example, by what the mathematician calls "planes."

Such topics are discussed in many informal logic texts and elsewhere. Two good sources are the following:

Max Hocutt, *First Philosophy,* Ch. 3
Howard Kahane, *Logic and Philosophy,* 4th ed., Ch. 12

Although we don't stop to define terms in many everyday situations, in most specialized disciplines definitions are frequently used. A major reason for their importance is that specialized disciplines use some common terms in special ways (for example, as physicists use the term 'elastic', steel and glass are highly elastic materials whereas rubber is not); or they use special terms—for example, 'quark' and 'ganglion'—not in ordinary language. Thus it is not uncommon in science, law, art history, music, and so on, for the discussion of some topic to begin with the definition of various terms. These definitions stipulate how the term will be used in that discussion (or explain how it is used in that discipline).

Some disciplines have even developed special types of definition. For example, in linguistics and computer science it is necessary to define the syntactic (grammatical) form of elements in the language such as statements, questions, arithmetic expressions, and identifiers. Various special notations have been developed for making such definitions rigorous yet succinct, like the "pictorial" notation called a "syntax diagram." (See, for example, Terrence W. Pratt, *Programming Languages,* 2nd ed., pp. 321–327, 449–450.)

Section 2: Instructions

Some of the exercises that follow discuss the inadequacy of a given definition—for example, 2–11. However, most of the exercises simply give a definition.

For the exercises in Section 2, do the following:

1. Examine each definition to determine what type it is: State whether the definition is reportive or stipulative.
2. Consider whether the definition is in any way defective or inadequate. Explain the faults in the definition. (In those exercises that discuss the inadequacies of some definition, consider whether all the claims are correct and whether there are any further critical comments that should be made about that definition.)

For example, consider the following statement:

'Filly' means young female horse, but in the rest of this work it will be taken to mean female horse under one year of age.

About this example the following comments are in order:

1. " 'Filly' means young female horse" is a reportive definition, stating how the term is used commonly in English. The remainder of the statement gives a stipulative definition of how 'filly' is to be understood in the work from which the passage is taken.
2. The stipulative definition is unproblematic. The reportive definition might be thought to be problematic as it is unclear how old a horse can be and still be considered young. It is not clear that this is a genuine defect of the definition because the term 'filly' as it is commonly used in English is probably similarly vague. However, the author clearly gave his stipulative definition to avoid the vagueness associated with how the word is normally used.

In some of the exercises of Section 2, there are missing use/mention quotes. Insert such quotes where they are required but not present.

Section 2: Exercises

2-1 Horace Dunkins, Jr., 19, pressed his hands down hard against the table in front of the judge's bench, and looked straight ahead yesterday as Circuit Judge Joseph Jasper sentenced him to die in the electric chair.

Before pronouncing sentence, Jasper read a written statement calling the rape and stabbing death of Mrs. Lynn McCurry an especially heinous, atrocious and cruel crime.

He said heinous as used by him means extremely wicked and shockingly evil, atrocious means outrageously wicked and vile, and cruel means inflicting a high degree of pain with utter indifference to the suffering it caused.

He said Mrs. McCurry was alive when she was stabbed 66 times, and that she died while being raped. ("Dunkins Sentenced to Chair," by Jane Aldridge, *Birmingham Post-Herald*, May 30, 1981, p. B6. Reprinted by permission.)

2-2 Feirstein divides the world into two kinds of people: real men and quiche eaters. Real men love John Wayne, chain saws, beer and *Monday Night Football*. They never call spaghetti "pasta," they never bunt, never have meaningful dialogues, and generally live lives of manly action. They are meat-and-potatoes men who are secure enough to wear their labels *inside* their clothing. They avoid foreign films because they are insufficiently violent and full of tired twaddle about the meaning of life. Quiche eaters, on the other hand, *never* see women as sex objects. They adore arugola salads, wear bikini underpants, gold chains and designer clothes, and in general are trendy, warm, sensitive wimps. They are forever sifting their psyches instead of doing something useful. Above all, they eat quiche, which real men avoid because it's French and looks as though it has already been eaten. Pete Rose is a real man. So is Margaret Thatcher, for sending the fleet to the Falklands. Robert Redford and Jerry Brown eat quiche. ("Of Real Men and Quiche Eaters," by John Leo, *Time*, August 23, 1982, p. 57. Copyright © 1982 Time Inc. All rights reserved. Reprinted by permission.)

*2-3 And the most common forms of running injury are knee injuries caused by pronation and supination, the side-to-side motion your foot makes when you run. (Ad for Converse running shoes, *Newsweek*, August 8, 1983, p. 13)

2-4 Dr. John Blackster, interviewed by Martin Redfern, on research conducted at the Scottish Marine Biological Association on the behavior of fish in the dark:

Redfern:
Do they actually sleep?

Blackster:
Well, we don't really know that. To some extent that depends on how you define 'sleep'. Certainly, their activity drops. In adult fish, the shoals—the adult herring shoals—break up, and they cease to respond to each other, and their swimming speed falls; so

that, if you could define 'sleep' as a reduction in activity, they certainly sleep. On the other hand, if you are thinking in terms of brain rhythms and human sleep, it's probably rather unlikely.

(BBC "Science Magazine," NPR, WBHM, January 15, 1984)

*2–5 NEW DEFINITION OF "MARRIED"

Generally, for rating purposes, married drivers who are under 30 years of age are in a different rate classification than unmarried drivers under 30 . . . Now State Farm has broadened the term "married."

Single persons shall be classified as married if they have custody of a minor child residing in their household. Widowed persons are also classified as married. (Explanatory news brochure from State Farm Insurance Companies, October 1983)

*2–6 Genuine literature must, by definition, be created by social outcasts and political exiles, misfits who remain marginal to officialdom and alienated from the state. In striving to retain their artistic integrity, writers condemn themselves to becoming heretics. ("Introduction, by Simon Leys," in *The Execution of Mayor Yin and Other Stories from the Great Proletarian Cultural Revolution,* by Jo-Hsi Chen, p. xviii)

2–7 As late as the 1930s, the word "computer" referred to a human being who performed mathematical calculations with the aid of a mechanical adding machine. By 1945, the word had a new meaning: a machine consisting of electronic components capable of high-speed manipulation and storage of information. (Advertising blurb from Greenwood Press for *Reckoners,* by Paul E. Ceruzzi)

2–8 When we say we want a module to be manageably small, we mean that a competent person would be able to take the listing of the module, read it, and keep a picture of its internal function in his head while deciding how to change it. (*Structured Systems Analysis: Tools and Techniques,* by Chris Gane and Trish Sarson, p. 184)

2–9 Acid rain is the term applied to acidic compounds formed when airborne pollutants, chiefly sulfur dioxide (a byproduct of burning coal) and nitrogen oxide (which comes mainly from cars), are changed chemically in the atmosphere and come to earth as dry particles or mixed in rain and snow. ("Academy Finds Direct Link Between Acid Rain and Aquatic Death," by Cass Peterson, *Washington Post* section, *Manchester Guardian Weekly,* July 10, 1983, p. 17)

2–10 "Culture " is a general term sociologists, anthropologists, and others use to refer to the whole collection of agreements that the members of a particular society share. (*Society by Agreement,* by Earl R. Babbie, p. 77)

2–11 What is a clam?

According to Webster, "any of various equivalve edible marine mollusks that live wholly or partly buried in sand or mud." Equivalve? One of the valves of the common steamer clam is bigger than the other. Edible? In the Puget Sound area *Schizothaerus nuttallii* is called the horse clam and declared uneatable (true, this is an error). Marine? The bent-nose clam survives far back from the sea in brackish water. Buried in sand or mud? The boring clam embeds itself in wood, cement or even rock. ("Clam," *Food: An Authoritative and Visual History and Dictionary of the Foods of the World,* by Waverly Root, p. 77)

2–12 While the exact details of the laws vary from state to state, most define your car as a lemon if in the first year of ownership one of two things occurs: The car has been to the dealer four times to have the same problem fixed, but the dealer has failed to repair it properly (it need not be the same dealer, just an authorized repair facility); or the car has been out of service for more than a total of 30 days due to one or more defects. ("Please Pass the Lemon Laws," *Consumer Reports,* November 1983, p. 609)

2–13 Any airtight container filled with food that has been sterilized by heat is technically considered a can, so a jar of food is a can, while a tin of ground coffee is *not* a can. (*The Big, Fertile, Rumbling, Cast-Iron, Growling, Aching, Unbuttoned Bellybook,* by James Trager, p. 348)

*2–14 Collards are on the list of soul food, a hazy category difficult to define except as whatever among edibles causes a Southerner far from home to grow misty-eyed. ("Collards," *Food: An Authoritative and Visual History and Dictionary of the Foods of the World,* by Waverly Root, p. 87)

2–15 Of course, concrete words as well as abstract ones get caught in this vortex of confusion. My favorite example is one I discovered while looking through a French dictionary many years ago. It defined *clocher* ("to limp") as *marcher en boitant* ("to limp while hobbling") and *boiter* ("to hobble") as *clocher en marchant* ("to limp while walking"). This eager learner of French was helped precious little by that particular pair of definitions. ("Metamagical Themas," by Douglas R. Hofstadter, *Scientific American,* April 1983, p. 21)

2–16 No family member may make decisions regarding hiring, promotion, salary level, job assignment, performance evaluations, discipline, or termination affecting another member of his/her immediate family.

Immediate family includes spouse, son or daughter (including step-children), grandchild, son- or daughter-in-law, parent (including step-parent), grandparent, father- or mother-in-law, brother or sister (including step-brother or step-sister), or brother- or sister-in-law. ("Nepotism," *You & UAB: Handbook for Administrative, Professional and Support Personnel,* p. 15)

2–17 A paperback is a book printed on cheap paper with an illustrated cardboard cover that usually misrepresents the story. ("My Lover, His Summer Vacation," *Dream Children,* by Gail Godwin, p. 91)

2-18 QUIZZLE

With this entry we offer the first of a regularly planned feature of *Theorist*. For those of you who don't know what a quizzle is, look it up in your dictionary. You didn't find it, right? That sums up a quizzle very nicely—you can't find the answer in a book. (*Theorist*, Fall 1983, p. 4)

2-19 "A supernova," said Ford as quickly and as clearly as he could, "is a star that explodes at almost half the speed of light and burns with the brightness of a billion suns and then collapses as a superheavy neutron star. It's a star that burns up other stars, got it? Nothing stands a chance in a supernova." (*Life, the Universe and Everything,* by Douglas Adams, p. 107)

2-20 The modern dream of energy wealth tends to inflate geometrically the possibilities of the land. Still, the resources available are significant, surely amounting to thousands of quads (one quad equals approximately 175 million barrels of oil, 60 million tons of coal, or 1 trillion cubic feet of natural gas) worth hundreds of billions of dollars. ("The Quad Mosaic—Energy and the Public Domain; A Cautionary History," by William K. Wyant, *Wilderness,* Winter 1983, p. 26)

2-21 One estimate has it that western energy development will require as much as 2.3 million acre-feet of water by the year 2000 (one acre-foot is enough water to cover an acre of land to the depth of one foot, or 253,000 gallons). ("Water to Burn," by T. H. Watkins, *Wilderness,* Winter 1983, p. 29)

2-22 "You're a Fascist, Wilbur. That's what you are."
"That's absurd," I said.
"Fascists are inferior people who believe it when someone tells them they're superior," she said.
"Now, now—" I said.
"Then they want everybody else to die," she said.
(*Slapstick, or Lonesome No More!* by Kurt Vonnegut, p. 122)

2-23 Let's pause and take a look at these failures in battle upon which Record rests his judgment of the military. In so doing I shall assume "battle" to mean a prolonged conflict between opposing military forces of considerable size, the outcome of which has considerable importance. ("Maligning the Military?" by Maxwell D. Taylor, *Washington Post* section, *Manchester Guardian Weekly,* February 19, 1984, p. 17)

2-24 The grocery industry as a whole is "mature," meaning that total sales volume is growing only slowly, if at all. ("Food Co-ops Face Tough Times," by Sam Zuckerman, *Nutrition Action,* March 1984, p. 8)

Section 3

Ambiguity, Homophony, Vagueness, Generality

Introduction

The examples of this section deal with various ways in which the meaning of a written or spoken piece of language can be unclear. The primary reason for lack of clarity is ambiguity; though vagueness, generality, and homophony—which are to be distinguished from ambiguity—can also be responsible.

Ambiguity

A word (or larger linguistic item such as a phrase or sentence) is ambiguous if it has two (or more) distinct meanings. For example, the word 'canon' has at least three different meanings:

1. a church decree or law
2. a type of musical composition
3. a certain position in the church hierarchy

Whereas all three uses of the term are associated with the church, the meanings are quite distinct, and thus the term 'canon' is ambiguous. (The word 'Canon' is a trade name of a type of camera, but because names don't have meanings, this is *not* a further way in which 'canon' is ambiguous.) Sometimes the ambiguity of a word will cause a sentence in which it occurs to be ambiguous. For example:

Pachelbel was responsible for five canons

could mean any of the following:

Pachelbel drafted five church decrees.

Pachelbel wrote five musical compositions of a particular type.

Pachelbel had in his charge five clerics holding a certain type of position in the church.

However, sometimes an ambiguous word will occur in a larger context that disambiguates the word—that is, the only way of making sense of the sentence is to understand the ambiguous term in one particular way. For example:

> *One of the canons that Pachelbel was responsible for went on to become pope*

is only intelligible on the assumption that in this sentence 'canon' has meaning 3.

When linguistic items larger than single words are ambiguous, it is important to distinguish term (or word) ambiguity from structural (or grammatical) ambiguity. 'Pachelbel was responsible for five canons' is an example of term ambiguity because the ambiguity of the sentence results from the ambiguity of a term in the sentence. However,

> *The children are ready to eat*

which can mean either

> *The children are ready to eat something*

or

> *The children are ready to be eaten*

is ambiguous, but not because some term in it is ambiguous. Rather, its ambiguity comes from the structure or grammar of the sentence.

Homophony

Two (or more) words are homophones when they sound the same (*homo* = same; *phone* = sound). For example, the words 'canon' (whose meanings we have just discussed) and 'cannon' (meaning a type of large gun) are homophones. (Thus a word can be both ambiguous and homophonous.) Clearly, because the same word can be pronounced somewhat differently in different dialects, what words have homophones varies from dialect to dialect (in the South 'earl' and 'oil' are homophones, and in many parts of Canada 'merry', 'marry', and 'Mary' are homophones).

Vagueness

A word is vague (or "open-ended") when its meaning is not completely precise. A good rule-of-thumb is that a word is vague if, no matter how much we know about it, we can't decide whether the word applies to some things. Most words in ordinary language are vague to some extent. A total lack of vagueness is generally only found in specialized contexts such as law and mathematics. For example, 'square' (meaning a closed, plane figure with four equal sides and equal internal angles) is completely without vagueness. 'Square' is, of course, also ambiguous, having the nineteen-sixtyish slang meaning of old-fashioned or not hip. So, properly speaking, it is a *meaning* of a term that is vague. Whereas 'square' in its mathematical meaning is not vague at all, this second meaning is very vague—it is impossible to specify exactly what is meant by 'square' in this slang usage, and it probably does not have a very precise meaning. The rule of thumb for detecting vagueness works here: Clearly, Governor George Wallace is square; equally clearly, the members of The Who are not; but it is very difficult to decide whether the term applies to a lot of others—people like Alan Alda, Dolly Parton, Teddy Kennedy, and Jane Fonda.

Generality

A word is general if there are other words that refer to specific subclasses of the things that the word refers to. Generality is a matter of degree—most words are general to some extent. 'Yellow' is more general than primrose-yellow, canary-yellow, lemon-yellow, and cream. But 'color' is more general than 'yellow'. It is important to distinguish ambiguity from generality. For example, 'record' can be used to refer to the accounts of a business or to a thin plastic disk that is played on a phonograph. But 'record' is not thereby ambiguous—these two different kinds of records are not sufficiently distinct for ambiguity. The noun 'record' refers to anything that preserves a trace or account of something that occurred in the past. So 'record' is general, phonograph records and accounting records being merely specific types of records. (However, it must be admitted that the distinction between ambiguity and generality is itself somewhat vague. We can see this in the vagueness of the word 'distinct' in our definitions of ambiguity as having two *distinct* meanings.)

Because ambiguity, vagueness, generality, and homophony (in the case of spoken language) can be responsible for unclarity, they can often be at the base of disputes and disagreements. It is therefore essential to be able to spot these features. Two books that discuss ambiguity in the context of arguments are the following:

Jerry Cederblom and David W. Paulsen, *Critical Reasoning,* pp. 56–61, 93

Howard Kahane, *Logic and Contemporary Rhetoric,* 4th ed., pp. 57–59, 210

Life would probably be a little more dull without some unclearness in language. As the examples that follow show, a lot of humor is based on ambiguity, homophony, generality, and vagueness. Moreover, the art of diplomacy would be considerably more difficult without these unclarities. However, the other side of the coin is that these features of language can mislead; and whether that is the intention, they often do contribute to advertisements and political statements misleading the unwary (see exercise 3–4). Also, these unclarities are one set of reasons why it is so difficult to produce computer programs that can translate from one natural language to another or respond in natural language to questions and commands in natural language. Artificial "computer languages" try to avoid the ambiguities and so on of natural language, although many such languages themselves have ambiguous expressions (see exercise 3–13).

Section 3: Instructions

A few of the exercises that follow simply discuss ambiguities and so on. Most, however, *are examples* of ambiguity, homophony, vagueness, and/or generality.

For each item in this section, do the following:

1. State whether the exercise involves ambiguity, homophony, vagueness, or generality. Check to determine whether more than one of these features occurs in the same exercise: (a) If the exercise involves an ambiguity, state whether it is term or structural ambiguity and explain all of the possible meanings (there may be more than two). (b) If the exercise involves homophony, give the words that are homophones. (c) If the exercise involves vagueness, say which word is vague and explain in what ways it is vague. (d) If the exercise involves generality, state what word is general and explain the different things to which it can refer.

2. Explain how the ambiguity, homophony, and so on, you have identified contributes to the passage. For example, if the passage is a joke, does, say, homophony contribute to the humor?

In your answers be careful to observe the use/mention distinction.

For example, consider the sentence

Eating bears can be dangerous.

This sentence involves ambiguity—in particular, structural ambiguity. It can mean either

Bears, when they are eating, can be dangerous (to passers-by)

or

Eating bear meat can be dangerous (to the eater).

The sentence is mildly amusing because it is unclear in which of two possible ways it is being claimed bears might be dangerous.

Section 3: Exercises

3–1 All employees who are not fired with enthusiasm soon will be. (Notice on office wall in UAB Medical Center, Summer 1982)

3–2 | SIN 4ME |

(Alabama car license tag)

3–3 | I LEFT MY ♥ IN SAN FRANCISCO |

| I ♥ SAN FRANCISCO |

(Bumper stickers)

3–4 Langendorf Natural Lemon Flavored Creme Pie contains no cream. It does contain sodium propionate, certified food colors, sodium benzoate, and vegetable gum.

That's natural?

Yes indeed, says L. A. Cushman, Jr., chairman of American Bakeries Co., the Chicago firm that owns Langendorf. The "natural," he explains, modifies "lemon flavored," and the pie contains oil from lemon rinds. "The lemon flavor," Cushman states, "comes from natural lemon flavor as opposed to artificial lemon flavor, assuming there is such a thing as artificial lemon flavor."

Welcome to the world of natural foods. . . .

In the midst of all this confusion, it's not surprising that the food industry is having a promotional field day. Companies are using various tactics to convince the consumer that a food product is "natural"—and hence preferable. Here are some of the most common:

The indeterminate modifier. Use a string of adjectives and claim that "natural" modifies only the next adjective in line, not the product itself. Take *Pillsbury Natural Chocolate Flavored Chocolate Chip Cookies.* Many a buyer might be surprised to learn from the fine print that these cookies contain artificial flavor, as well as the chemical antioxidant BHA. But Pillsbury doesn't bat an eyelash at this. "We're not trying to mislead anybody," says a company representative, explaining that the word "natural" modifies only "chocolate flavored," while the artificial flavoring is vanilla. Then why not call the product "Chocolate Chip Cookies with Natural Chocolate Flavoring"? "From a labeling point of view, we're trying to use a limited amount of space" was the answer. (Copyright 1980 by Consumers Union of United States, Inc., Mount Vernon, N.Y. 10553. Reprinted by permission from *Consumer Reports,* July 1980)

3–5 Dear Stepmother: There must be a special place in heaven reserved for people like you, but I hope you don't have to wait that long for your reward. Bless you for your generous, understanding heart. ("Dear Abby," *Birmingham News,* November 20, 1981, p. 14C)

3-6   Once, a movie magazine, preparing a profile article on actor Cary Grant, sent a telegram to him asking

HOW OLD CARY GRANT?

To which Cary Grant replied with a telegram saying

OLD CARY GRANT FINE. HOW YOU?

("All Things Considered," NPR, WBHM, January 18, 1984)

3-7   Tony Roberts talks about his first time.

Roberts:
It was exactly seven years, eleven months, two weeks and five days ago, at 7:00 P.M. on Fire Island.

Interviewer:
You remember the exact moment?!

Roberts:
Of course. A man never forgets his first time.

Interviewer:
It must have been quite an experience. You must tell me about it!

Roberts:
I was at a beach party comparing tan lines, when an exotic woman in a red sarong sauntered over in my direction. I immediately noticed that she had the best tan on the beach.

Interviewer:
Go on.

Roberts:
She looked me straight in the eye and said, "Campari?" "I'm sorry," I replied, "I don't speak Italian." "Neither do I," she said. I was so embarrassed.

Interviewer:
I can see why!

Roberts:
Anyway, she handed me a Campari and orange juice, and sipped a Campari and soda herself. Then I understood.

Interviewer:
How was it?

Roberts:

At first I thought it was bitter. Then I realized it was sweet, too. I guess bittersweet is the only way to describe it.

Interviewer:

Was she amused?

Roberts:

Very. She said, "You'll acquire a taste for it, Tony. Most men do." She was right. My second time was much better. And now I like to have it as often as I can.

Interviewer:

Did you ever see the young woman again?

Roberts:

No, but I keep hoping I will. I've enjoyed it so many ways since my first time . . . now I could teach her a thing or two.

(Ad for Campari, *Omni*, June 1982, p. 19. Reprinted by permission.)

3-8 SOUTHERN BAPTIST PASTORS IMPROVING BY DEGREES (Headline, *Alabama Baptist*, January 5, 1984, p. 1)

3-9 CITY MAY IMPOSE MANDATORY TIME FOR PROSTITUTION (Headline, *Tampa Tribune*, August 7, 1979)

*3-10 MAYDAY M'Aidez

3-11 CHEMISTS HAVE SOLUTIONS
(Bumper sticker)

3-12 "How dare you belch in front of my wife!"
"Sorry, old man, I didn't know it was her turn."
(Dialogue from the film *Sir Henry at Rawlinson End*)

3-13 FORTRAN syntax provides another example [of ambiguity]. A reference to A(I,J) might be either a reference to an element of the two-dimensional array A or a call of the function subprogram A, because the syntax in FORTRAN for function calls and array references is the same. Similar ambiguities arise in almost every programming language. (*Programming Languages: Design and Implementation*, by Terrence W. Pratt, 2nd ed., p. 307)

3-14

(Graffito on the wall of a men's restroom)

3–15 "This coffee tastes like mud."

"That makes sense. It was just ground this morning."

("You can't do that on T.V.," *Nickelodeon*, September 1983)

*3–16 Q: What animals are in banks?

A: Your bucks and your doe.

(Joke from a book of riddles in a box of Cracker Jacks)

3–17 | NURSES ARE PATIENT PEOPLE |

(Bumper sticker)

3–18 "Being short never bothered me for three seconds . . . the rest of the time I wanted to commit suicide." (Mel Brooks, quoted in review of *The Height of Your Life*, by Ralph Keyes, *Newsweek*, May 12, 1981, p. 94)

3–19 Taste that beats the others *cold!* (Pepsi advertisement)

3–20 The Sierra Club was instrumental in the reelection of Sen. Robert Stafford (R-Vt.), who, as chair of the committee, has been a staunch advocate of air-pollution and acid-rain controls. ("1983: A Look Back at the Year's Most Important Environmental Events," by David Gancher, *Sierra*, January/February 1984, p. 34)

3–21 | LIBRARIANS ARE NOVEL LOVERS |

(Bumper sticker)

3–22 We will curl up and dye for you. (Sign outside Fashion Flair Beauty Salon & Beautique, Shades Crest Road, Bluff Park, Alabama, October 1982)

3–23 FEDERAL OFFICIAL CITES 20 YEARS OF PROGRESS IN MENTAL RETARDA-TION. (Headline, *UAB Report*, November 25, 1983, p. 2)

3–24 A soprano is a woman with smooth sailing on the high C's. ("Picturesque Speech," *Reader's Digest*, December 1981, p. 153)

3–25 IRAQIS REPULSE IRANIANS (Headline, *Birmingham Post-Herald*, July 19, 1982, front page)

3–26 WHEN IT POURS IT REIGNS

Raingo do-it-yourself solid vinyl gutter and downspout systems

Raingo reigns supreme over all other gutter systems. (Ad for Raingo gutter systems, *Reader's Digest*, May 1982, p. 58)

3–27 America's biggest doughnut company. (Advertisement)

3–28 King Arthur:

I hear you've been misbehaving.

Knight:
In what manor, sire?
("Towards More Picturesque Speech," from the *Rotarian,* quoted in *Reader's Digest,* May 1982, p. 39)

3-29

> Did you wake up GROUCHY this morning,
> or did you let her sleep?

(Bumper sticker)

*3-30   Our Foods Not So Hot (Advertisement for Pedro's, Birmingham, Alabama)

3-31   Wherever four Catholics are gathered together there is always a fifth. (A Catholic priest at a meeting of the Alabama Philosophical Society, November 4, 1978)

3-32   Bill Cosby's First Law of Economics: "Every man's income runs into four figures: the real one, the one he reports to the IRS, the one he tells his wife, and the one he tells the guys at the club." ("Chatter," by Michael Small, *People,* June 13, 1983, p. 126)

3-33   Two cannibals are having dinner together. The guest says to his host, "Your wife sure makes good soup."

   "Yeah, but I'm going to miss her," his friend replies. (*Truly Tasteless Jokes,* by Blanche Knott, p. 105)

*3-34   After some revision of these designs, an extensive critique was again held, leading to the final selection in 1979 of a design [for the programming language] that subsequently was named "Ada" (after Ada Lovelace, an early pioneer in computing). Whittaker [1978] gives a more extended history of the early development of Ada. (*Programming Languages: Design and Implementation,* 2nd ed., by Terrence W. Pratt, pp. 457–458)

3-35   "You'd better be prepared for the jump into hyperspace. It's unpleasantly like being drunk."
   "What's so unpleasant about being drunk?"
   "You ask a glass of water."
   Arthur thought about this. (*The Hitchhiker's Guide to the Galaxy,* by Douglas Adams, p. 59)

3-36   Nearing completion [at Houston's First Baptist Church] is the Christian Life Center, featuring two full-sized basketball courts, a roller rink, six bowling lanes, four glassed-in racquetball courts, a suspended jogging track, saunas, whirlpool baths and a restaurant called The Garden of Eatin. ("The Superchurches of Houston," by David Gates and Daniel Shapiro, *Newsweek,* October 24, 1983, p. 117)

3-37   The Reformation happened when German nobles resented the idea that tithes were going to Papal France or the Pope thus enriching Catholic coiffures. ("A History of the

Past: 'Life Reeked with Joy,' " compiled by Anders Henriksson, *Wilson Quarterly,* Spring 1983, p. 169)

3–38 The Wilsons' house was on Philip Street, a street so rich it even had its own drugstore. Not some tacky chain drugstore with everything on special all the time, but a cute drugstore made out of a frame bungalow with gingerbread trim. Everything inside cost twice as much as it did in a regular drugstore, and the grown people could order any kind of drugs they needed and a green Mazda pickup would bring them right over. The children had to get their drugs from a fourteen-year-old pusher in Audubon Park named Leroi, but they could get all the ice-cream and candy and chewing gum they wanted from the drugstore and charge it to their parents. ("Rich," *In the Land of Dreamy Dreams,* by Ellen Gilchrist, p. 14)

3–39 GET A PART-TIME JOB IN OUR BODY SHOP.

It feels great to work your body into top condition. To push it to the limit. And then exceed it. . . .

In the Guard, you'll train to keep your body in condition while you practice your military skills. (Ad for the Army National Guard, *Gentlemen's Quarterly,* September 1983, p. 169)

3–40

(T-shirt design)

Section 4

Connotation and Assertive Content

Introduction

Arguments are often presented in an attempt to influence a person to accept a certain conclusion. However, things other than arguments can influence people's opinions: One of them—connotation—is the subject of the examples in this section.

Two (or more) words can have the same assertive content but very different connotation. For example, saying that a person is thrifty and saying that she is miserly is saying basically the same thing—that she saves, is careful about how she uses valuable commodities, and so on. But 'thrifty' and 'miserly' have very different connotation. We would use 'thrifty' in describing a person if we wished to express approval; and in contrast, we would use 'miserly' if we wished to express disapproval. 'Thrifty' has *positive* connotation, whereas 'miserly' has *negative* connotation.

Sometimes the difference in connotation between two words that have the same assertive content is not obviously linked to approval and disapproval. 'Blended' and 'mixed', when used to describe whiskey, have the same assertive content but different connotation. 'Blended' suggests a degree of care and attention that is not suggested by 'mixed'—and therefore 'blended' has positive connotation whereas 'mixed' is neutral with respect to connotation. Of course, there is some approval and disapproval connoted by these terms as in the mixing of whiskies care and attention is thought to be desirable.

A good rule of thumb for determining when two (or more) words differ only in connotation is that the only difference between them is that one is used to express greater or lesser approval than the other. Few words differ only in their connotation. However, connotation is often a more important criterion in the choice of a word than is assertive content.

The connotation of words is a very important feature of language. Other things being equal, we might feel more inclined to buy a whisky that is advertised as blended rather than one advertised as mixed. Although 'Thrifty' might be suitable as a name for a car-rental business, 'Miserly' is probably not. The switch to the name 'EXXON'—chosen partly because of its connotations (the double "X" was at the time very unusual in English, suggesting exclusivity)—is reported to have cost Standard Oil of New Jersey approximately $100 million—and it isn't likely that the company made the switch expecting to lose money. (See Howard Kahane, *Logic and Contemporary Rhetoric,* 2nd ed., p. 100.)

Very often people choose words with a particular connotation to elicit our support for some position or cause instead of giving reasons or arguments why we should support it. Proponents of abortion tend to refer to an unborn human as a fetus, whereas opponents tend to refer to it as a child or baby. Both are attempts to influence opinion in favor of their view without giving reasons for that view. In a similar way, opponents and proponents of euthanasia describe the same person as, respectively, a living human being and a human vegetable. Scientists often describe animals that are killed as an integral part of a research project as having been sacrificed. Pictures are often used in a similar attempt to sway our opinion without reasons. Exercise 4–19, which clearly attempts to elicit our support for a cause by the use of words with strong connotation, is the text that accompanies pictures of fluffy, pure-white baby seals leaving trails of blood across pristine snow—not a pretty picture but *in itself* hardly a reason to oppose the seal hunt.

It is essential to be able to detect the use of words with strong connotation to *dis*count their effect if we are to correctly assess the reasons *for* some conclusion. This is the rationale for considering connotation before we take up the topic of the assessment of arguments.

Two informal logic texts that discuss connotation are the following:

Howard Kahane, *Logic and Contemporary Rhetoric,* 4th ed., Ch. 5
Gerald M. Nosich, *Reasons and Arguments,* pp. 154–155.

Section 4: Instructions

Four of the following exercises, 4–3, 4–8, 4–15, and 4–17, discuss the use of words with strong connotation. For these exercises

1. Explain why the words mentioned in these passages were chosen rather than different words with the same assertive content.

The other exercises in this section are passages that contain words with strong connotation. In these exercises

1. Underline the words in each passage that, by their connotation, might influence a person's view.
2. Rewrite the passage to change its point of view by using words with different connotation, but retaining all and only those facts already in the passage.

For example, if the given passage read

Inflation has spiraled 2 percent in the past month, while at the same time unemployment has soared to 12 percent

it should be marked up to give

Inflation has <u>spiraled</u> 2 percent in the past month, while at the same time unemployment has <u>soared</u> to 12 percent.

The passage can be rewritten to give a very different impression:

During the course of the whole of the past month, inflation has only inched up by 2 percent, while unemployment has risen only to 12 percent.

The use of words with strong connotation occurs in some exercises in earlier sections. See, particularly, some of the exercises in Section 2. You should be alert for this feature of language when assessing arguments in subsequent sections.

Section 4: Exercises

*4-1 *James Michener's U.S.A.* is bubble-headed from the first page to the last. By contrast, even Michener's leaden, interminable novels are works of art. This book aims to exploit his popularity and gives his readers nothing of value in return—unless you count 17 pictures of James A. Michener, which is the number to be found herewith. By turns, he looks kindly, public spirited, grandfatherly and wise: by lending his name to this enterprise, he also looks greedy. ("Rummaging in America's Attic," by Jonathan Yardley, a review of *James Michener's U.S.A.*, *Washington Post* section, *Manchester Guardian Weekly*, January 24, 1982, p. 18)

4-2 One of the wig-making villains lathered my face for ten terrible minutes and finished by plastering a mass of suds into my mouth . . . Then this outlaw strapped his razor on his boot, hovered over me ominously for six fearful seconds, and then swooped down upon me like the genius of destruction . . . Then the incipient assassin held a basin of water under my chin . . . with the mean pretense of washing away the soap and blood. ("Parisian Shave," *The Comic Mark Twain Reader*, ed. Charles Neider, p. 76)

4-3 It's interesting to observe the kind of language being used . . . to chronicle the unhappy goings-on in the South Atlantic.

Nothing terribly new about this. Paul Fussell, in his book *The Great War and Modern Memory*, drew up his own list of poetic and euphemistic language used in that conflict. A few examples: a horse was a *steed* or *charger*; to conquer was to *vanquish*; the front was the *field*; warfare was *strife*; to die was to *perish*; the army was the *legion*; the dead were the *fallen* . . .

The last few days have turned up a list just as impressive as Fussell's Great War catalogue . . . a few examples: The Union Jack is *The Flag of Freedom*: the South Atlantic is the *cruel waters*; British soldiers are *our brave boys*; British commandos are *our tough guys*.

The language is unashamedly discriminatory. British casualties tend to be the *price of victory*, which doesn't seem to be true of Argentine casualties. Sea Harriers tend to be *lost* or *shot down*; while Mirages and Skyhawks are, as a general rule, *blown out of the sky*. Argentine gunboats, by the same formula, are *blasted* to smithereens while British ships are generally *sunk*.

Britain's "brave planes" carry out bombing raids or strafe enemy ships; Argentine pilots, by contrast, embark on *desperate suicide missions* or carry out *merciless air onslaughts*. And talking of "brave planes," you may have noticed that HMS Antelope . . . was a *brave little frigate*, not so much blasted to smithereens as *stricken*. ("Guardian Diary," *Manchester Guardian Weekly*, June 6, 1982, p. 19. Reprinted by permission.)

4-4 An unidentified general surgeon talking about what he called "skin incisions" that he makes during surgery: "I *never* cut people." ("All Things Considered," NPR, WBHM, October 5, 1983)

*4–5 British Airways has moved to shore up its sagging finances by offloading two of its new Boeing 757 jet aircraft almost two years before they are delivered from the manufacturers. In a highly complex deal, British Airways is to allow Air Europe, the charter and package tour arm of Intasun Leisure, to take over two of the 19 new 757s. The arrangement will save the struggling state-owned airline around £40 million and ease the burden of meeting the £400 million cost of the original 757 package.

The deal follows strenuous efforts by BA management to "reschedule" the 757 deal, by taking delivery of the new jets over four years instead of the planned three. ("British Airways Offloads Two 757s," *Washington Post* section, *Manchester Guardian Weekly,* July 11, 1982, p. 17. Reprinted by permission)

4–6 I was educated some in chemistry, and in biology and physics, too, at Cornell University. I did badly, and I soon forgot all they tried to teach me. The Army sent me to Carnegie Tech and the University of Tennessee to study mechanical engineering—thermodynamics, mechanics, the actual uses of machine tools, and so on. I did badly again. I am very used to failure, to being at the bottom of every class.

An Indianapolis cousin of mine, who was also a high school classmate, did very badly at the University of Michigan while I did badly at Cornell. His father asked him what the trouble was, and he made what I consider an admirable reply: "Don't you know, Father? I'm dumb!" It was the truth.

I did badly in the Army, remaining a preposterously tall private for the three years I served. ("Triage," *Palm Sunday,* by Kurt Vonnegut, pp. 73–74)

4–7 It is not pleasant to see an American thrusting his nationality forward *obtrusively* in a foreign land, but Oh, it is pitiable to see him making of himself a thing that is neither male nor female, neither fish, flesh, nor fowl—a poor, miserable, hermaphrodite Frenchman! ("A Sort of People," *The Comic Mark Twain Reader,* ed. Charles Neider, p. 89)

4–8 George Orwell was right. And he was really right in Washington, the city that christened the MX the "Peacekeeper." Or how about "revenue enhancement," President Reagan's favorite name for a tax increase? Or the "district work period," which is congressional Newspeak for vacation? And "protective reaction"? That's what Richard Nixon called the invasion of Cambodia, where they didn't drop bombs but instead engaged in "air support." As a matter of fact, when did you last hear the word "bomb"? A country now explodes a "nuclear device," which is placed aboard a "re-entry vehicle," which is also an "RV"—not to be confused with a "recreational vehicle," which is a Winnebago. War itself is now a "nuclear exchange," which sounds like high-technology gift-giving. ("Newspeak—Washington Version," by Elizabeth Bumiller, *Washington Post* section, *Manchester Guardian Weekly,* September 18, 1983, p. 16. Reprinted by permission)

*4-9 We've overdone teaching the academics and ignored the need for vocational training. I think the universities have to get more into the practical aspects of teaching graduates how to do something while they are in attendance, so that when they leave, they already have done what they are hoping to do for the rest of their lives. I call it an action-oriented curriculum. (Jerry Falwell, quoted in "The Nutshell Interview," *Nutshell*, Fall 1981, p. 38)

4-10 There is a real and present danger that an intellectual fraud may soon be inflicted on Alabama's public school children by legislation. The fraud in question is cleverly misnamed "scientific creationism."

Even more serious, however, than the possible imposition of this piece of pseudo-science is the fact that a pack of non-scientists (i.e., state legislators) would have the gall to decide (in part, at least) what is to be taught as science by science instructors in public schools. This kind of presumption poses the gravest threat to the integrity of American science since the infamous Scopes monkey trial of 1925.

The very idea that it could happen again should send a chill up the spines of scientists and science educators throughout our state. The comic opera spectacle of politicians debating as to whether or not an ancient Semitic creation myth (told around Bedouin campfires late in the Stone Age) deserves equal time with modern scientific theories of cosmic, planetary and biological evolution makes us the laughing stock of the civilized world. Such an absurdity should be resisted implacably, if not for truth and the integrity of science, then for patriotic purposes. . . .

Let those who love truth and science rise up and smite this outrage and may God have mercy on those who would perpetrate intellectual fraud on our children.

(Letter by Rev. Emmett O. Zondervan, D.D. " 'Scientific Creationism' Is Clever Fraud," *Birmingham News*, March 9, 1981)

4-11 A monkey seated in a chair is taught to distinguish visually between a series of circles and squares. After being irradiated with 500 to 600 rads, the monkey is then watched to determine . . . how badly his skills have degraded. Before most animals become too sick to perform, they are "sacrificed," according to AFRRI scientists. ("Pentagon Boffins Experiment for World War III," by Rick Atkinson, *Washington Post* section of *Manchester Guardian Weekly*, July 1, 1984, p. 17)

4-12 The British Government's decision to reject the Brandt Report should be warmly welcomed. Someone from a position of authority and influence had to put the boot in sooner or later. Unctuous and high minded, embodying the usual neocolonialist aspirations of the aid lobby and the development mafia, the Report was already beginning to assume a venerated status of the kind customarily reserved for tablets in stone.

Enlightened people in the First World, who ought to have known better, fell for its progressive verbiage, ignoring the obvious fact that it was peddling the same old developmentalist nostrums that have characterized discussions about the world economy for the last two decades. Now, at least, a forthright statement from the British Foreign Office reiterating the colonial (rather than the neocolonial) arguments that continue to flower in the West (and where Mrs. Thatcher leads can Ronald Reagan be far behind?), may serve to stop the Brandt bandwagon dead in its tracks. ("Destroy the System," by Richard Gott, *Manchester Guardian Weekly*, August 3, 1980, p. 8. Reprinted by permission.)

4-13 Now, after nearly three years of Sandinista rule, Nicaragua has assumed the trappings of a Marxist military dictatorship. The promise of free elections has been ignored. Human rights are being grossly violated by a government that terrorizes, imprisons and kills without compunction. Political pluralism has become a sick joke—nine Marxist commandantes, heavily influenced by Cuba, wield the only real power. The government has seized key industries—banking, foreign exchange, fisheries and mining—and its daily threats to seize more are strangling the once-booming economy. By some estimates, more than 100,000 Nicaraguans have fled their country since the FSLN takeover. ("Nightmare in Nicaragua," by Ralph Kinney Bennett, *Reader's Digest*, May 1982, p. 47)

*4-14 Margaret Thatcher, née Roberts, was a dreadful child who grew into a dreadful woman. So prissy was she that classmates would devise circuitous routes to school to avoid meeting her on the way. Fellow students at Oxford detected an unattractive tendency to manipulate people. At her first job, as a chemist in a plastics factory, she was nicknamed "Duchess" because she was so haughty. Denis liked her but his parents shared the general unfavorable view. Her only recorded hobby is interior decorating. ("Coffee-table Thatcher," by Michael Leapman, a review of *Margaret Thatcher: Wife, Mother, Politician* by Penny Junor, *Manchester Guardian Weekly*, October 23, 1983, p. 21)

4-15 The word "catastrophe" resonates with apocalyptic hopes and fears. One thinks of atom bombs, cosmological big bangs, black holes, political terrorism, airplane crashes, earthquakes, floods, fires, revolutions, third encounters, and the Second Coming. Catastrophe theory! What PR expert could have devised a better name? Had Thom called it "discontinuity theory" it is likely that only mathematicians would have learned of it.

Because any abrupt change that springs from a confluence of smoothly changing variables can be described by a catastrophe model, it follows that CT can invade any branch of science. ("Four Books on Catastrophe Theory," *Science: Good, Bad and Bogus,* by Martin Gardner, p. 369)

4-16 The concealed story behind the American aggression against Grenada is not one of British incompetence or craven complicity but concerns the extent and the depth of the Anglo-American rift.

Mrs. Thatcher would have nothing to do with a lawless act of intervention against a small Commonwealth country. . . .

In the heightened atmosphere of the renewed party battle at Westminster the American aggression against Grenada has been treated as an issue affecting national pride and prestige. That is a trivial consideration compared with the international implications of the event. There is nothing novel about Washington failing to consult with the ally; it seldom does when the policy-making bureaucracy moves to panic stations at the time of crisis management. What is most ominous about the affair is the trigger-happy mood which has gripped the Reagan Administration in the wake of recent setbacks and disasters. ("The Forebodings That Follow Grenada," by Peter Jenkins, *Manchester Guardian Weekly,* November 6, 1983, p. 9. Reprinted by permission.)

4-17   In the bad old days of nutritional theory—up to 1970, say—dietary fibre was usually known as roughage. School matrons used it as mildly punitive therapy to scour their charges' insides but *bona fide* nutritionists who had test-tubes and cages full of rats were for the most part unimpressed. After all, they said, roughage was no more than the cell walls of plants; and everyone knew that plant cell walls were made of cellulose, and that cellulose was inert, like argon and polythene, and was therefore undigested. . . .

Hugh Trowell, in 1972, coined the term that seems now to have been in the language forever: "dietary fibre." . . .

Hugh Trowell's concept of "dietary fibre" is similar, in essence, to the old-fashioned concept of "roughage": that proportion of the diet that is not digested by enzymes of the mouth, stomach, or small intestine, and which therefore reaches the colon in pristine form—and so, by implication, is not absorbed. ("The Ins and Outs of Roughage," by Colin Tudge, *New Scientist,* June 21, 1979, pp. 988–989. Reprinted by permission)

4-18   Rhetoric is much too genteel a word. What is presently passing between the Superpowers is nothing less than raucous abuse, with Mrs. Thatcher's ideological caterwauling lately thrown in for good measure, as if further measure were needed. ("Russia in the Real World," by John Erickson, *Manchester Guardian Weekly,* October 16, 1983, p. 21)

4-19   CAUTION

The photos enclosed show scenes from the baby seal massacre. You will find them extremely disturbing.

Please read my letter to you before deciding to open this insert.

These shocking photos were taken by Brian Davies, executive director of IFAW.

IFAW is pledged to end this terrible treatment of animals. With your immediate involvement we pledge to do all that we possibly can to stop the torment that seals like these are suffering. (Text from an International Fund for Animal Welfare pamphlet, January 1983).

4-20   Sullivan:

The Chinese refer to it as a "personal responsibility system," which is a marvelous phrase. It's been applied mostly in the countryside. A personal responsibility system means you can decide whether you want to grow rice or cotton, and if cotton is a better crop to grow—you can get a better price for the cotton than you can for rice—then you get to reap the profits and if you guess wrong you have to bear the responsibilities for the losses.

Angle:
The Chinese have even extended the personal responsibility concept to industry, threatening to close down factories that don't make a profit.

(Newscaster Jim Angle and Roger Sullivan, executive vice president of the National Council for U.S.–China Trade, talking about a new Chinese economic system. "All Things Considered," NPR, WBHM, January 11, 1984)

4–21 Key architects of Secretary Watt's resource-giveaway programs are still running the show at the Interior Department, with no signs that they will be removed. (Denny Shaffer, president of the Sierra Club, quoted in "Clark's Interior: Another Fox in the Henhouse?" *Sierra*, January/February 1984, p. 20)

4–22 Dialogue from a Wee Pals cartoon strip:

Frame 1: Sybil:
"In your article about Ralph running for hallmonitor, you refer to Ralph's "friends," Oliver."

Frame 2: Oliver:
"Sure, what's wrong with that Sybil?"

Frame 3: Sybil:
"Are we for or against his nomination?"

Oliver:
"We're against him."

Frame 4: Sybil:
"Change 'friends' to 'cronies.' "

(*Ann Arbor News*, March 13, 1980, p. B11)

4–23 No more heavy clodhoppers to lug around. Rocky Weatherbeaters are featherweights at an average of only 27 oz. a pair! (Ad for Rocky Weatherbeater hiking boots, *Sierra*, September/October 1982, p. 13)

4–24 The horny composer in *10* was Moore's breakthrough performance; the lusty, immature heir to multimillions in *Arthur* enshrined him. . . . Some other movies in the same general period have been nonhits—*Wholly Moses, Six Weeks, Lovesick* and *Romantic Comedy.* ("Dudley Moore: Not Just a Joker," by Byron Laursen, *Ampersand*, February/March 1984, p. 12)

Section 5

Simple and Compound Sentences

Introduction

The exercises in this section give you practice in recognizing the component simple sentences in compound sentences.

There are four basic types of compound sentences:

Conjunctions

The standard form of a conjunction is two sentences joined together with 'and'. For example:

Pasta comes from China and sashimi comes from Japan

is a conjunction formed by placing 'and' between the two component sentences 'Pasta comes from China' and 'Sashimi comes from Japan', which are called "conjuncts." Although they all have slightly different uses, there are many other words that can be used instead of 'and' to form a conjunction. Some of these words are: but, however, although, yet.

Very few conjunctions occur in the standard form. Usually, a conjunction is contracted in some way, though it can be rewritten, without change of meaning, in the standard form. Some examples are as follows:

Turnip greens and pecan pie are southern dishes.

Fried green tomatoes are tasty yet they are found only in the South.

Sometimes the word joining up the two conjuncts of the conjunction can occur at the beginning of a sentence:

Although spaghetti alla carbonara is easy to prepare, it is served in few restaurants.

Sometimes the conjunction is emphasized by including the "noise word" 'both' along with 'and':

Chips and fried-fish both taste best when doused in malt vinegar.

Although the basic form of a conjunction is two sentences joined by 'and', three (and more) sentences can be so joined:

Calvin Trillin, Fats Goldberg, and Chairman Mao all love greasy food.

Where conjunctions of more than two sentences occur, they can be thought of as composed of one conjunction formed from two arbitrarily selected sentences—for example:

Calvin Trillin loves greasy food AND Fats Goldberg loves greasy food

and another conjunction formed by conjoining this compound sentence to the remaining sentence:

(Calvin Trillin loves greasy food AND Fats Goldberg loves greasy food) AND Chairman Mao loves greasy food.

Disjunctions

The standard form of a disjunction is two sentences (the disjuncts) joined together with 'or'. As in the case of conjunctions: (1) Disjunctions are often contracted: (2) Disjunctions can be expressed using 'unless': (3) 'Unless' can occur at the beginning of the sentence: (4) The "noise word" 'either' can occur in a disjunction: (5) There can be disjunctions with more than two disjuncts. The following are all disjunctions:

Eating rhubarb leaves or Angel of Death mushrooms can cause sickness.

Unless cranberries had been an Indian food, they would never have a place on the Thanksgiving menu.

Fresh blueberries should be served with cream, either whipped or liquid.

Today's soup du jour is minestrone, vichyssoise, or gazpacho.

Conditionals

The standard form of a conditional is 'if' followed by a sentence (the antecedent), followed by 'then', followed by another sentence (the consequent). For example:

If Olga is an Algerian then Olga's children will have tasted couscous.

Often conditionals are contracted in various ways. Frequently the 'then' is omitted (sometimes its absence is indicated by inserting a comma). The preceding conditional might be stated more naturally as

If Olga is Algerian, her children will have tasted couscous.

'If' and the antecedent don't have to occur at the beginning of the sentence.

Olga's children will have tasted couscous if she is Algerian

is another variant of this conditional. The sentence that follows 'if' is always the antecedent, except where 'if' occurs as part of the expression 'only if', in which case the sentence that follows 'only if' is the consequent:

Only if her children have tasted couscous is Olga an Algerian.

There are other ways of expressing conditionals, some of them not using the word 'if'. These variants are too numerous to list here, but one example is

Were Olga to be an Algerian, her children would have tasted couscous.

Negations

Unlike conjunctions, disjunctions, and conditionals, which join two component sentences to form a compound sentence, the compound sentences called 'negations' contain an operator on one component sentence. For example:

It is not the case that french fries are a balanced food

contains the component sentence 'French fries are a balanced food' operated on by 'it is not the case that', which negates the component sentence. Usually, the negating is done by the word 'not' (or some contraction of it) occurring within the sentence being negated. For example:

Egg yolks are not free of cholesterol.

Truffles aren't cheap.

Whereas conjunctions, disjunctions, conditionals, and negations are the basic building blocks of compound sentences, complex examples of compound sentences may contain them all. For example:

If today is Christmas Day or Thanksgiving then most Americans are eating turkey but not pizza.

This sentence is basically a conditional, where its antecedent is the disjunction 'Today is Christmas Day or Thanksgiving' and the consequent is a conjunction of 'Most Americans are eating turkey' and the negation of 'Most Americans are eating pizza'.

Two books with discussions of the distinction between simple and compound sentences are the following:

Patrick J. Hurley, *A Concise Introduction to Logic,* pp. 12–13 and Ch. 6.1

Howard Kahane, *Logic and Philosophy,* 4th ed., Ch. 2

The distinction between simple and compound sentences is fundamental in propositional logic (the topic of Section 11). Also, being able to identify the component parts of a compound sentence is important in distinguishing the parts in an argument. Although the component parts of disjunctions, conditionals, and negations don't need to be distinguished outside of propositional logic, sometimes in the analysis of arguments conjunctions need to be broken down into their component conjuncts.

Section 5: Instructions

Analyze the compound sentences that follow.

1. Mark up the passages in the book in the following manner: (a) Underline the words joining together two (or more) component sentences or operating on sentences. (b) Insert angle brackets (< . . . >) around the simple sentences (or fragments of simple sentences) that occur in the passage.

2. Write out the compound sentence in its standard form—as two component sentences joined by 'AND', 'OR', or 'IF . . . THEN . . . ' or as a sentence preceded by 'NOT'. (Write these words for operators in all upper-case letters to distinguish them from the component sentences.) If one of the component sentences is itself compound, write the component compound sentence within a set of parentheses to indicate this fact.

For example:

If today is Christmas Day or Thanksgiving then most Americans are eating turkey but not pizza

should be marked up to yield

If <today is Christmas Day> **or** <Thanksgiving> **then** <most Americans are eating turkey> **but not** <pizza>.

This should then be rewritten as

IF (Today is Christmas Day OR Today is Thanksgiving) THEN (Most Americans are eating turkey AND (NOT Most Americans are eating pizza))

Section 5: Exercises

5-1 While some Italian wines are produced from single grape varieties, many are made from precisely specified mixtures of grapes. ("Italian Wines—Some Facts," *Italian Wine Guide*, p. 1)

5-2 Alabama is at a crossroads. We can move forward, stand still or fall backward. We can elect a leader who fits the times and has a common sense approach to government; or we can continue to be distracted by shallow, simplistic political rhetoric. (George McMillan campaign literature, Fall 1982)

*5-3 I can either run this hotel or look after Tallulah Bankhead. I can't do both. (Frank Case, quoted in *Miss Tallulah Bankhead*, by Lee Israel, p. 47)

5-4 Although these imposing landmarks survive in mint condition, Copenhagen has never lived in the past. ("Cozy, Captivating Copenhagen," by Christopher Lucas, *Reader's Digest*, May 1982, p. 156)

5–5 The main distinction between psychology and sociology, then, is one of emphasis with psychology emphasizing the personal and sociology emphasizing the interpersonal. (*Society by Agreement*, by Earl R. Babbie, p. 14)

5–6 It's a very funny thought that, if Bears were Bees,
They'd build their nests at the *bottom* of trees.
And that being so (if the Bees were Bears),
We shouldn't have to climb up all these stairs.
(*Winnie-the-Pooh*, by A. A. Milne, p. 6)

5–7 The label may just say "vegetable oil," but it is no health bargain unless it is neither coconut nor palm oil. (*Jane Brody's Nutrition Book*, by Jane E. Brody, p. 80)

5–8 They [Canadian pigs] grow fast, are free of both swine fever and hog cholera, and taste good. ("Two Little Pig Stories," *Canada Today/d'aujourd'hui*, September 1982, p. 4)

5-9 Financial aid is being cut, and tuition is skyrocketing. Either we get knocked out by a one-two punch, or we get up and fight back. (Janice Fine, quoted in "Campus Chronicle," *Nutshell*, Fall 1982, p. 7)

5-10 On sunny days, the northern fur seals do not go to the water, but stay on the beach. (Ansel Blake, quoted in "How Sea Mammals Beat the Heat," *Sierra*, September/October 1982, p. 82)

*5-11 Unless we dramatically improve funding for education, and in particular teacher salaries, our children and their children will not have the opportunity for the quality education that was ours. ("The Educated Militant," *RSA Advisor*, February 1984, p. 2)

5-12 Wolfgang Pauli and other scientists have begun to study the role of archetypal symbolism in the realm of scientific concepts. ("Science and the Unconscious," by M. -L. Franz, in *Man and His Symbols*, by Carl G. Jung et al., p. 381)

5-13 Although four Surveys have been conducted prior to 1975, *RW* traces the Survey's origin to that first year of ranking shoes. ("8th Annual Runner's World Special Shoe Survey," *Runner's World*, October 1982, p. 43)

5-14 Nature will castigate those who don't masticate. (Horace Fletcher, quoted in *Food: An Authoritative and Visual History and Dictionary of the Foods of the World*, by Waverley Root, p. 125)

5-15 If he hears a clash between instruments, he isolates the offenders and prints their scores on the screen, spots the problem and corrects it. ("Chips Off the Old Bach," *Canada Today/d'aujourd'hui*, September 1982, p. 2)

5-16 If you or your group is interested in organizing a fundraising event for Oxfam America, Special Events Coordinator Moli Steinert can be consulted for ideas, guidance, and written materials on how to produce successful special events. ("Events Against Hunger," by Moli Steinert, *Oxfam America News*, Winter 1984, p. 6)

5–17 By advertising in the Bell System Yellow Pages you're doing yourself a favor. (*Greater Birmingham Yellow Pages*, August 1983, p. 432)

5–18 *If currently employed, avoid moving and relocating,* if possible. ("Are You Prepared for 1985?" by K. Neil Earle, *Plain Truth*, March 1984, p. 37)

5–19 To fully enjoy your coffee, plan on drinking it within a half hour after it's brewed; the flavor remains at optimum levels for at least that long, particularly if the temperature is held at about 180 to 190 degrees (F). *(The Coffee-Lover's Guide to Beans, Blends and Brewing)*

*5–20 A map in your ad will help people find you. (*Greater Birmingham Yellow Pages*, August 1983, p. 67)

5-21 Try always to strike with precision, otherwise you will end up leaving "moons" in the wood. (*Illustrated Basic Carpentry*, by Graham Blackburn, p. 89)

5-22 Where the press is free and every man able to read, all is safe.—Thomas Jefferson ("Quotable Quotes," *Reader's Digest*, May 1982, inside front cover)

5-23 He knows that, to solve these problems, we must put an end to the old style of negative politics that has gotten us nowhere. (George McMillan campaign literature, Fall 1982)

5-24 If the drawings from Tycho's records as reproduced by Drayer are the *same size* as those made at Hveen, and *if* the "foot" used by Kepler and Tycho is nearly equal to our contemporary measure, *then* there is confirmation in Tycho's pictures of the eclipse of 1598 that he and his assistants used the "correction factor" method. ("Kepler, Tycho, and the 'Optical Part of Astronomy': The Genesis of Kepler's Theory of Pinhole Images," by Stephen Straker, *Archive for History of Exact Sciences*, 1981, p. 281)

*5–25 Buster and Mr. Lewis been knowing each other for a long time. (*Buster Holmes Handmade Cookin'*, p. 79)

5–26 It's guaranteed to cook up light and fluffy every time, or its makers will refund your money. (Ad for Success rice, *Reader's Digest*, May 1982, p. 193)

5–27 The notion of a feature detector was well established by Barlow and by Hubel and Wiesel, and the idea that extracting edges and lines from images might be at all difficult simply did not occur to those who had not tried to do it. (*Vision: A Computational Investigation into the Human Representation and Processing of Visual Information*, by David Marr, p. 16)

5–28 At the end of the hour he finally asked, "May questions about Aristotle's rhetoric be asked?"

"If you have read the material," he was told. (*Zen and the Art of Motorcycle Maintenance*, by Robert M. Pirsig, p. 361)

5-29 Pitt Street, Adolf found, was in the Chinese quarter of the city, below the unfinished cathedral. (*Young Adolf,* by Beryl Bainbridge, p. 158)

5-30 The corridor is permanently illuminated, and when the intruder's shadow falls over the photocell detector hidden in the floor an alarm bell is set ringing. (*Seeing: Illusion, Brain and Mind,* by John P. Frisby, p. 15)

5-31 If I had behaved well [in prison] and seemed generally reasonable, and if there could be no suspicion at all about my bodily health and vigor, and if my hair was really light, and my eyes blue and my complexion fresh, I was to be sent up at once to the metropolis in order that the king and queen might see me and converse with me; but . . . when I arrived there I should be set at liberty, and a suitable allowance would be made. (*Erewhon,* by Samuel Butler, p. 52)

5-32 One of Buster's friends is Woody Allen who stopped in to eat red beans and rice at the Buster Holmes Restaurant and to jam with a few of the boys hanging around who had their instruments with them. (*Buster Holmes Handmade Cookin',* p. 73)

5-33 Few Latin Americans spoke English or French, few Canadians Spanish or Portuguese. ("Canada and the Countries to the South," *Canada Today/d'aujourd'hui*, 1983, No. 6, p. 2)

5-34 And if the gargoyles would have put Francis Bacon off his lunch, then it was clear from the gargoyles' faces that the statute would have put them off theirs, had they been alive to eat it, which they weren't, and had anybody tried to serve them some, which they wouldn't. (*Life, the Universe, and Everything*, by Douglas Adams, p. 122)

5-35 He [Guy] couldn't get into the army, navy, marines, or air corps. ("Summer, an Elegy," *In the Land of Dreamy Dreams*, by Ellen Gilchrist, p. 155)

5-36 The Forest Service has full authority to adjust or cancel the long-term contracts with LP and ALP . . . If this is done *and* the legislative mandate for a high cut is repealed by Congress, *and* the cut on native corporation lands is included in future logging targets, *and* the residual pricing system is reformed to recover management costs in timber sales—then perhaps a better era will beckon. ("Mandate for Oblivion: Saying Goodbye to the Rain Forest—And Paying for the Privilege," by Thomas J. Barlow, *Wilderness*, Spring 1984, p. 34)

Section 6

Simple and Serial Argument Forms

Introduction

This section begins the actual examination of arguments. The examples provide exercise in distinguishing arguments from nonarguments and in identifying two sorts of argument structures.

In logic 'argument' is used to refer to a piece of reasoning that gives a reason (or reasons) for some conclusion. In this context 'argument' has none of the connotation of dispute and disagreement that the term sometimes has when used in everyday situations.

Identifying Arguments

In analyzing arguments it is essential to be able to differentiate reasons from conclusion. The way to do this is to ask which sentence or sentences, if they were true, would give reason for believing another of the sentences to be true. The sentence or sentences that give the reasons are the premises or reasons in the argument. The sentence supported by the given reasons is the conclusion.

Certain indicators are very helpful in distinguishing reasons from conclusions. Some words (or longer expressions) typically indicate that the conclusion immediately follows the word (and that at least part of the premises will usually have preceded the word). Such words are called conclusion indicators. Some examples follow:

Conclusion Indicators
therefore
thus
so
hence
it follows that
which shows that
which proves that
from which one can conclude that

Some words typically indicate that one or more reasons immediately follow the word—these are called reason indicators. Some examples follow:

Reason Indicators

because
since
for
for the following reasons

Although these examples are some very common conclusion and reason indicators, there are many other words and expressions that can be used for the same purposes.

Indicator words are useful, but they don't guarantee correct identification of the parts of an argument. Some arguments contain no indicator words; some of the words that sometimes occur as inference indicators (for example, 'for' and 'since') other times have different uses; and sometimes the author of an argument (the person giving or presenting the argument) will purposely use them in places where they should not be used in an attempt to give the impression that he has given an argument when, in fact, he has not. Thus, identifying the premises and conclusion of an argument by the use of indicator words should always be checked subsequently by the more fundamental criterion of what sentence or sentences in the passage give reasons for accepting what other sentence.

Simple Arguments

The simplest argument structure—called, appropriately, the simple argument structure—is where one reason is given for one conclusion. The following is a simple argument:

Zaphod has two heads, so he needs two hats.

Here 'so' is a conclusion indicator; the conclusion 'He [that is, Zaphod] needs two hats' immediately follows 'so', and the reason 'Zaphod has two heads' immediately precedes it. The reason does not have to come before the conclusion in a passage:

Arthur didn't want them to build the bypass because it would mean the destruction of his house.

In this sentence the conclusion comes at the beginning of the passage, followed by 'because', which is immediately followed by the reason. Reason and conclusion don't have to be separated by an indicator word, but if there is no indicator word separating them, there may often be punctuation instead:

Because Ford was an intergalactic hitchhiker, he was not ruffled by the destruction of Earth.

In this argument 'Ford was an intergalactic hitchhiker' is the reason, as is suggested by the position of 'because'. Finally, there may sometimes be no indicator words in an argument:

> *The Pan Galactic Gargle Blaster is the most powerful drink in the universe—it would knock the socks off one of Pat O'Brien's Hurricanes.*

Here it is best to construe 'The Pan Galactic Gargle Blaster is the most powerful drink in the universe' as the reason, because it gives strong support to 'The Pan Galactic Gargle Blaster would knock the socks off one of Pat O'Brien's Hurricanes', whereas the latter does not strongly support the former.

Serial Arguments

The serial argument structure is two simple arguments where the conclusion of one of the simple arguments is the reason in the other. The following is a serial argument:

> *Forty-two is the answer to the biggest question in life; so, the biggest question in life* might be *"What's 7 times 6?"; thus, the biggest question in life* might be *a mathematical question.*

Everything up to the second semicolon in the sentence is one simple argument—'Forty-two is the answer to the biggest question in life' is the reason for concluding 'The biggest question in life *might be* "What's 7 times 6?"'—and this latter sentence is itself the reason in the simple argument whose conclusion is 'The biggest question in life *might be* a mathematical question'. So this is a serial argument whose *basic reason* (the reason in the "first" simple argument) is everything up to the first semicolon, *whose intermediate conclusion* (the conclusion of the "first" and the reason of the "second" argument) is the sentence between the two semicolons, and whose *final conclusion* (the conclusion of the "second" argument) is the sentence after the second semicolon. As in the case of simple arguments, the component parts of serial arguments don't have to occur in any particular order in the passage, and they might not be accompanied by indicator words. For example:

> *Ford was lucky enough not to have to spend the whole of his life on Earth; because, as a researcher for* The Hitchhiker's Guide to the Galaxy, *he had to travel from planet to planet.*

'Because' immediately following the semicolon indicates that what comes before the semicolon is the conclusion, the remainder of the sentence being the reason for that conclusion. But the remainder of the sentence is itself an argument whose reason comes before the comma and conclusion after it. Thus overall the passage is a serial argument with basic reason 'Ford was a researcher for *The Hitchhiker's Guide to the Galaxy*', intermediate conclusion 'Ford had to travel from planet to planet', and final conclusion 'Ford was lucky enough not to have to spend the whole of his life on Earth'.

Two texts that discuss the preceding points in more detail, using analysis techniques similar to those outlined in the following instructions, are as follows:

Stephen N. Thomas, *Practical Reasoning in Natural Language*, 2nd ed. Ch.1–1 to 1–3

Monroe C. Beardsley, *Practical Logic*, Ch.1

Section 6: Instructions

Some of the examples that follow are arguments, others are not (that is, none of their component sentences is a reason for any other). If the example is not an argument, simply state that fact. In the case of examples that are arguments, analyze them by doing the following:

1. Mark up the passage by (a) circling inference indicator words and (b) putting angle brackets around, and numbering, component significant sentences (or sentence fragments). Significant sentences may be simple or compound sentences.

2. For any sentence fragment (or sentence that is unclear because it contains pronouns and so on), specify the complete sentence beneath the passage, including the complete sentence in angle brackets and numbering it with the number of the corresponding sentence fragment in the passage.

3. Draw an argument diagram showing the structure of the argument. The diagram consists of the numbers of the significant sentences and arrows. Each arrow represents an argument link, with the reason at the tail of the arrow and the conclusion at the head. Simple and serial arguments will be diagramed as follows:

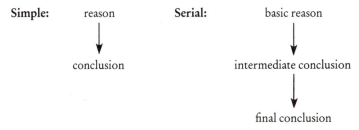

(It is customary, though not essential, that arrows point down the page.)

4. Next to the argument diagram, state the type of argument structure of the argument.

For example, the passage

Arthur was an Englishman, hence he liked warm beer

should be marked up to yield

< ①Arthur was an Englishman >, (hence) < ②he liked warm beer. >

Sentence ② needs further specification because of the pronoun 'he' in it; so beneath the passage we write

< ②Arthur liked warm beer >

and we give a diagram

Simple

For example:

< ① Zaphod had to have two pairs of contact lenses > (because) < ② he had two heads >; (hence) , < ③ looking after his eyes cost him twice as much as it cost the average contact lens wearer. >

< ② Zaphod had two heads >

< ③ Looking after his eyes cost Zaphod twice as much as it cost the average contact lens wearer >

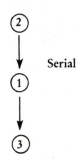

Serial

Section 6: Exercises

6–1 You feel you never left the ground

Because we treat you like dirt.

(Caption at the end of a "commercial" for Trans-Eastern Airlines, "Saturday Night Live," September 11, 1982)

6–2 More doctors recommend Cortaid for dermatitis and minor itches and rashes for one important reason: nothing you can buy without a prescription works better than Cortaid to relieve itching caused by eczema, insect bites, mild poison ivy, poison oak, poison sumac, allergies, soaps and detergents. (Ad for Cortaid, *Good Housekeeping*, July 1983, p. 212)

*6–3 The 1850s and 1860s were boom decades [in Britain]. British exports grew more rapidly in the first seven years of the 1850s than in any other period of the nation's history. (*Algeny*, by Jeremy Rifkin, p. 70)

6-4   I do it because I do it, because that's what I do. (Werner Erhard, the originator of est, quoted in "Powers of Mind," *Science: Good, Bad and Bogus,* by Martin Gardner, p.304)

6-5   At eleven-thirty that night, Candy had another bath—a bubble bath this time steeped with pine-fragrance crystals—and put on the black nightgown she had bought for the occasion. Finally, a fresh application of Tabu, and, by five minutes to midnight, she was in her bed, the lamp a glowing rose, and soft music purring from the radio. (*Candy,* by Terry Southern and Mason Hoffenberg, p. 39)

6-6   Fat, however, contains more than twice as many calories per ounce as carbohydrates (including sugar) or proteins. Thus, a pat of butter on a slice of toast is more than twice as fattening as an equal weight of jelly. ("Sweet Truths About Sugar," by Elizabeth M. Whelan and Fredrick J. Stare, M.D., *Reader's Digest,* October 1983, p. 139)

6-7   I am a poet: I am always hungry. *(Straw for the Fire: From the Notebooks of Theodore Roethke 1943-63,* selected by David Wagoner, p. 179)

6-8 It's an impossible task, therefore interesting. (Stewart Brand, quoted in "Capturing the World of Software," *Time*, July 18, 1983, p. 70)

6-9 Care Bears bring out the best in kids. Care Bears inspire your youngster to play in a caring way. Because Care Bears are specially designed with feeling in mind. (Ad for Care Bears, *Working Mother,* June 1983, p. 39)

*6-10 L'Anse- aux-Meadows is probably Vinland. It is, at any rate, the only authenticated site of a Norse Viking settlement in North America. ("Remains to Be Seen," *Canada Today/d'aujourd'hui,* June 1983, p. 3)

6-11 I don't want everyone to like me; I should think less of myself if some people did.—Henry James, *The Portrait of a Lady* ("Quotable Quotes," *Reader's Digest,* May 1982, inside front cover)

6–12 Conserving the planet's tropical areas is especially important to realizing the utilitarian benefits of wild species. Some 70 percent of the Earth's plants and animals exist in the tropics. ("By Saving Wild Species, We May Be Saving Ourselves," by Norman Myers, *The Nature Conservancy News*, November/December 1983, p. 7)

6–13 Herald:
I am happy; I no longer ask the gods for death.

("Agamemnon," *The Complete Greek Tragedies: Vol. 1, Aeschylus*, p. 51)

6–14 Since a subprogram represents an abstract operation, we should be able to understand its specifications without understanding how it is implemented. (*Programming Languages: Design and Implementation*, 2nd ed., by Terrence W. Pratt, p. 129)

6–15 I don't like a man to be too efficient. He's likely to be not human enough.—Felix Frankfurter ("Quotable Quotes," *Reader's Digest*, May 1982, inside front cover)

6–16 The final appearance of any project depends just as much on how it is fastened together as on the kind of leather and the shapes of the different pieces. Choosing an appropriate means of fastening is therefore one of your primary concerns. *(Things to Make with Leather: Techniques & Projects, p. 21)*

6–17 Please join us today, like so: Get a pen. Check and initial the "membership application" form that your hand is touching. Tear off the Interim Membership stub, sign and pocket it, and wait six weeks or so for your first magazine and permanent card. (Letter from Nancy C. Mackinnon, soliciting memberships in the Nature Conservancy, September 1983, p. 3)

6–18 Quite simply, humanity is about to view nature in temporal terms because it is now beginning to engineer the entire temporal life span of living things. (*Algeny*, by Jeremy Rifkin, p. 219)

6–19 Of course we know that people do not get rich by being good, and that is the reason why so many of you people try to get rich some other way. ("Address to the Prisoners in the Cook County Jail," Clarence Darrow, in *Philosophy and Contemporary Issues*, 3rd ed., eds. John R. Burr and Milton Goldinger, p. 63)

6-20   It tastes so good, you forget the fiber. (Ad for Post Fruit & Fibre cereal in *Reader's Digest*, May 1982, p. 219)

*6-21   The *pop* operation cannot be applied to the empty stack because such a stack has no elements to delete. Therefore, before applying the *pop* operation to a stack, we must ensure that the stack is not empty. (*Data Structures Using Pascal*, by Aaron M. Tenenbaum and Moshe J. Augenstein, p. 60)

6-22   Because we don't have 4 years to waste.
Elect McMillan governor
(George McMillan campaign literature, Fall 1982)

6-23   We love because it's the only true adventure.—Nikki Giovanni, in *Ebony* ("Quotable Quotes," *Reader's Digest*, May 1982, inside front cover)

6–24 Bacardi dark.

It tastes good mixed because

It tastes good unmixed.

(Ad for Bacardi rum in *Newsweek*, March 16, 1981, p. 9)

6–25 WHY DRIED FOODS?

When food is dehydrated or freeze dried, the water is removed, making the food lightweight and compact . . . (Recreational Equipment, Inc., catalog, Spring 1984, p. 65)

6–26 May is such a nice month—you wouldn't think it would have Mondays.—Charles Barsotti, Long Island, N.Y. (*Reader's Digest*, May 1982, p. 85)

6–27 The popularity of leather sandals . . . leather wallets, belts, purses, luggage and clothing is attested to by the many leather shops, craft fairs, and boutiques selling leather goods. (*Things to Make with Leather: Techniques & Projects*, p. 5)

6-28 There was no European language that Ruth could not speak at least a little bit. She passed the time in the concentration camp, waiting for death, by getting other prisoners to teach her languages she did not know. Thus did she become fluent in Romany, the tongue of the Gypsies. (*Jailbird*, by Kurt Vonnegut, p. 16)

6-29 Suddenly they heard a clattering chop-chop-chop in the distance. "Helicopter!" Terry whooped. "They've found us!" ("We're Dying Down Here!" by Glenn Joyner, *Reader's Digest*, May 1982, p. 75)

*6-30 The simplest things can present problems. André must use a pencil to dial a telephone, because his fingers won't fit the holes in the dial. ("A Giant Among Us," by Terry Todd, *Reader's Digest*, May 1982, p. 117)

6-31 I long to be a greater failure in life so I can write better books. (*Straw for the Fire: From the Notebooks of Theodore Roethke 1943–63*, selected by David Wagoner, p. 178)

6-32 An unoccupied home also requires more heat than might be expected because the normal usage of appliances and lights when the home is occupied tends to generate extra heat in the home. ("Questions & Answers," *Pipeline*, January 1984, p. 5)

6-33 Fat makes the heart work harder since each extra pound of body fat requires about one quarter mile of blood vessels. It is obvious, therefore, that you cannot acquire the highest level of physical efficiency when you are overweight. (*The Royal Canadian Air Force Exercise Plans for Physical Fitness*, p. 63)

6-34 I was only six years old when they dropped the atomic bomb on Hiroshima, so anything I remember about that day other people have helped me remember. (*Cat's Cradle*, by Kurt Vonnegut, p. 18)

6-35 Cars are so small these days that a pedestrian has to look left, right and down.—Doug Larson ("Towards More Picturesque Speech," *Reader's Digest*, May 1982, p. 39)

6-36 Having financed the ship from his own shares in the company and with much of his own fortune, Stephen was hardly a rich man any longer. ("Stephanie, Stephen, Steph, Steve," *Quotations from Other Lives,* by Penelope Gilliatt, p. 26)

6-37 He [Canadian Prime Minister, Pierre Trudeau] is also concerned that new intercontinental strategic weapons may be so highly mobile as to be virtually invisible, and it might consequently be impossible for either side, or for international bodies, to verify arms control agreements. ("Prime Minister Pierre Trudeau Addresses Peace and Security," *Canada Today/d'aujourd'hui,* special edition, Winter 1983, p. 4)

6-38 Dear Heloise: Living alone has its compensations . . . at least you get to lick the bowl when baking!—Jack DuPree (" Heloise," *Birmingham News,* January 4, 1984, p. 2B)

6-39 He [Slartibartfast] had been planning to learn to play the octaventral heebiephone, a pleasantly futile task, he knew, because he had the wrong number of mouths. (*Life, the Universe and Everything,* by Douglas Adams, p. 106)

6-40 Not knowing telephone numbers is a problem since there is no operator service. ("The Lebanon Diaries," by Sandy Smith, *Blue Note*, January 1984, p. 6)

6-41 I have an *Encyclopaedia Britannica* here in the lobby of the Empire State Building, which is the reason I am able to give Dostoevski his middle name. (*Slapstick, or Lonesome No More!* by Kurt Vonnegut, p. 91)

6-42 It [Compound 1080] is odorless and tasteless and thus cannot be detected when impregnated in meats or dissolved in liquids. ("EPA and the Politics of Poison: The 1080 Story," by Jim Sibbison, *Defenders*, January/February 1984, p. 6)

6-43 This heating season we expect no increase in the cost of gas we purchase from our supplier and, consequently, no price increases to our customers. ("Questions & Answers," *Pipeline*, January 1984, p. 1)

6-44 By 1800 the international community of scientists had become quite large, and its means of communication through journals and extensive systematic private correspondence were well established. Thus, it was possible for many physicists to contribute to the understanding of electromagnetic phenomena. (*Physics for Poets*, by Robert H. March, p. 87)

6-45 Sexual progeny have a multitude of different genes, and therefore different characteristics, so the odds are better that at least a few will survive any significant change in their environment. ("Why Sex?" by Gina Maranto and Shannon Brownlee, *Discover*, February 1984, p. 24)

6-46 Because he has not held elective office, there is little in Jackson's career or record to indicate his positions on key environmental issues. ("The Democratic Candidates and the Environment," *Sierra*, March/April 1984, p. 35)

6-47 When Father Quixote opened his eyes he was surprised to see that the countryside was in rapid motion on either side, while he lay quietly in almost the same position as the one in which he had fallen asleep. Trees pelted past him and then a house. He supposed his vision had been affected by the wine which he had drunk. (*Monsignor Quixote*, by Graham Greene, p. 151)

6-48 "I think it's going to be a very good election, since we have three people running," he [Jimmy Wooten, chairman of the Student Government Association Election Commission] said. ("Three UAB Students Bid for UC-SGA Presidency," *Kaleidoscope*, April 10, 1984, p. 1)

Section 7

Convergent, Divergent, and Linked Argument Forms

Introduction

The examples of this section are arguments of three further forms.

Convergent Arguments

In the convergent argument structure, two reasons are given to support the same conclusion. For example:

> *Arthur Hailey's books are to be found at airport newsstands and supermarket checkouts, and several of his novels have been made into films; so he must be a popular novelist.*

Here two separate reasons are given for the conclusion 'Arthur Hailey must be a popular novelist'—one of the reasons being 'Arthur Hailey's books are to be found at airport newsstands and supermarket checkouts' and the other, 'Several of Arthur Hailey's novels have been made into films'. In this argument, as in all convergent arguments, each reason supports the conclusion independently of the other reason; thus convergent arguments are essentially two simple arguments that have the same conclusion. Using the techniques introduced in the instructions in Section 6, convergent arguments can be represented as follows:

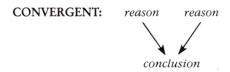

CONVERGENT: *reason*   *reason*

conclusion

Notice that in treating the argument about Arthur Hailey as a convergent argument, the compound sentence from the beginning of the passage to the semicolon (the reasons) has been split into its two conjuncts, and each of these conjuncts is considered to be a separate reason. We could have left this compound sentence as one reason—and thus have considered the argument to be a simple argument. However, doing this would have failed to display the fact that two quite different reasons are given for the conclusion. So it is preferable to interpret this argument as convergent. Notice also that even treating it as a convergent argument with two reasons, one of those reasons is expressed in a compound sentence (from the beginning of the passage to the first comma). We could separate this conjunction into its component conjuncts and consider the argument to be an argument with *three* reasons convergent on the same conclusion. It is a matter of judgment whether to treat this argument as having two or three independent reasons: Our assessment is that the facts that the books are available in airports and supermarkets are sufficiently similar that they are not different reasons—they just both point to the wide availability of his books. However, the facts that the books are widely available and that some have been made into movies are sufficiently different to be considered independent reasons. (Books that are available at airports are generally available at supermarkets; but many such books—for example, Harlequin romances—are never made into films: a fact for which everyone should be grateful!) Whereas there is often a question of whether conjunctions should be split into their component parts as different significant sentences in an argument, other types of compound sentences should not be decomposed into their simpler elements but should always be treated as one significant sentence.

Divergent Arguments

In the divergent argument structure, the same reason is a reason for two different conclusions—the inverse of the situation with the convergent form. For example:

> *Because Richard Yates is not a popular author, he probably can't sell advance movie rights for his books, and one can expect not to see his face on the cover of* Newsweek.

'Richard Yates is not a popular author' is the reason here for the two different conclusions. Again, we could treat these two conclusions as one compound conclusion; but because the contents of the two claims are fairly different, the structure of the argument is best exposed by analyzing the argument as divergent. Like convergent arguments, divergent arguments can be seen essentially as two simple arguments that have the same reason. Divergent arguments can be represented as follows:

DIVERGENT:

reason

conclusion   conclusion

Linked Arguments

The linked argument structure is like the convergent as it involves two reasons and one conclusion. But whereas the reasons in the convergent structure are *independently* reasons for the conclusion, in the linked structure each reason taken by itself is not a reason for the conclusion, but *taken together* they do provide support for the conclusion. For example:

> *Barbara Pym's novels are about Anglican clerics. No novels about Anglican clerics are as exciting as John Le Carré's spy stories. So none of Barbara Pym's novels are as exciting as John Le Carré's spy stories.*

The two reasons in this argument are given in the first two sentences. By itself, neither of these reasons supports the conclusion; taken together, however, they furnish strong support for the conclusion. To indicate that it is only the reasons taken together that support the conclusion, linked arguments are diagramed as follows:

LINKED:

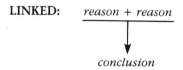

In practice, it is sometimes very difficult to decide whether an argument is linked or convergent. There are some especially difficult cases where both reasons do independently support the conclusion, but the sum of the amount of support they give independently is less than the amount of support they give to the conclusion when taken together. In such cases, because our interest is to represent the argument being analyzed as favorably as possible, the argument should be represented as linked. This slightly complicates the account of the linked argument structure, which is more adequately stated as follows: An argument is linked when its two premises taken together give more support to its conclusion than the sum of the supports that each premise individually gives to the conclusion.

As in the case of simple and serial arguments, so in the case of convergent, divergent, and linked arguments, the premises and conclusions of the argument don't have to occur in any particular order in the passage, and indicator words may or may not be present.

We have discussed the simplest forms of convergent, divergent, and linked argument structures. However, they are all generalizable further: A convergent argument can have more than two reasons for its one conclusion, a divergent argument more than two conclusions drawn from the same premise, and a linked argument more than two premises that when taken together support the conclusion. Similarly, in Section 6 we presented only the simplest case of the serial argument: A serial argument can be composed of any number of simple arguments, so long as the conclusion of one is the premise of the next, the conclusion of that argument is the premise of the one following that, and so on.

The same texts referred to in Section 6 for their coverage of simple and serial argument forms also explore convergent, divergent, and linked argument forms:

Stephen N. Thomas, *Practical Reasoning in Natural Language*,
2nd ed., Ch. 1–1 to 1–3

Monroe C. Beardsley, *Practical Logic*, Ch.1

Section 7: Instructions

Analyze the following arguments according to the directions for the analysis of arguments given in the instructions in Section 6. If you feel there is more than one way in which the argument could be construed (for example, as a convergent or as a linked argument), choose what you think is the best interpretation to make your analysis, and if you think it is necessary, write a brief note after the argument diagram explaining why the way you analyzed the example is preferable to the alternative you considered.

Here is one example:

< ① Joseph Heller is the author of the widely read book *Catch-22*>, < ② a novel that includes such unforgettables as Colonel Cathcart and the maid in the lime-green panties>— (so) , < ③ Heller is responsible for many people remembering Cathcart and the maid in the lime-green panties. >

< ② *Catch-22* is a novel that includes such unforgettables as Colonel Cathcart and the maid in the lime-green panties>

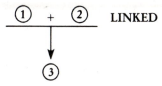

Another example is the following:

< ① People's huge appetite for tasteless jokes > (suggests that)< ② Blanche Knott can expect to become rich from her publications> and < ③ the reading public can expect *Truly Tasteless Jokes Three, Truly Tasteless Jokes Four, . . .*>

< ① People have a huge appetite for tasteless jokes>

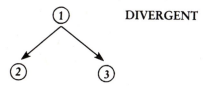

Section 7: Exercises

7-1 Before both baking and barbecueing, we recommend parboiling . . . 2 to 4 minutes, which not only removes unwanted fat but makes the end result more palatable. ("About Spareribs," *Joy of Cooking*, by Irma S. Rombauer and Marion Rombauer Becker, p. 481)

*7-2 AMERICANS GETTING TOO SALTY

Only one gram of sodium a day is enough to sustain the human body in normal health, say researchers at the University of Massachusetts in Amherst.

Unfortunately, they report, the average American consumes between 5 and 15 grams of sodium in table salt each day. (*Star*, February 20, 1979, p. 7)

7-3 I had gathered, even then, that he [Sir Quentin] had plans for inducing me [Fleur Talbot] to write more compromising stuff into these memoirs, but I had no intention of writing anything beyond what cheered the boring parts of the job for the time being and what could feed my imagination for my novel *Warrender Chase*. So that his purposes were quite different from mine. (*Loitering with Intent*, by Muriel Spark, p. 37)

7-4 *THE BEST SIX-CYLINDER CAR IN THE WORLD*

THE SIX- CYLINDER ROLLS-ROYCE

The most graceful,

the most silent,

the most flexible,

the most attractive,

the most reliable,

the most smooth running,

in fact,

The best six-cyclinder car yet produced.

(Text of 1907 ad for Rolls-Royce cars, an illustration in "Henry Royce: The Humble Mechanic Who Built the World's Best Motor Car, " by G. N. Georgano, *This England*, Autumn 1983, p.44)

7-5 Californians also do pretty well in conserving their money and the nation's resources. In April of this year California had 10 percent of the nation's population, drivers, and automobiles. Yet Californians used only 9.5 percent of the nation's gasoline that month. (Letter by M. D. Murphy, *Birmingham News*, November 29, 1979)

7-6 I watch laundromat washers the way other people watch television, it's soothing because you always know what to expect and you don't have to think about it. (*The Edible Woman*, by Margaret Atwood, p.96)

7-7 Macro lenses are misnamed. When used alone most will produce only a half-life-size image, which is not in the photomacrography range. ("The Low-Down on Closeups," by Jon R. Nickles, *Sierra*, November/December 1982, p. 46)

7-8 In a telephone conversation with the *Washington Post*, John W. Hinckley Jr. said he likes being in St. Elizabeth's Hospital for the mentally ill: Nobody bothers him, they call him Mr. Hinckley and people began asking for his autograph as soon as he arrived. ("Hinckley's Autograph," *Birmingham Post-Herald* , July 5, 1982, p. A4)

7-9 Since Titan appears red, and we view it at the cloud deck, there must, according to this argument, be red clouds on Titan. ("Titan, The Enigmatic Moon of Saturn," *Broca's Brain: Reflections on the Romance of Science*, by Carl Sagan, p. 185)

*7-10 Two important points have been clearly identified by the Soviet attack on KAL Flight 007: 1. The Soviets do not recognize individual rights; 2. The Soviets cannot be trusted.

Wayne Morgan Caverly
Pierrefonds, Quebec, Canada
(Letter, *U.S. News & World Report*, September 26, 1983, p. 7)

*7-11 There are two main reasons why someone might buy a six-month bank certificate instead of going for the higher yields of a money-market fund. The first is that these certificates are insured by an agency of the federal government. The second is that a certificate enables you to lock up your 9 percent, or whatever rate you are getting for the next six months. ("A Guide to High-Yield Investments," by Richard Blodgett, *McCall's*, July 1980, p. 78)

*7-12 The New Balance 990 is the most technologically sophisticated running shoe made today.
       It has a unique polyurethane Motion Control Device for maximum stability. A midsole unit made of three different layers of EVA for shock absorption. And a *new* Superflex outersole with a carbon rubber heel pad for durability. (Ad for New Balance running shoes, *Sports Illustrated*, September 5, 1983, p. 57)

7-13 Well, Tab isn't by our pompous standards, an "educated" man . . . I mean he doesn't have the robe and scrolls, and he doesn't speak in polysyllables. (Professor Mephesto in *Candy*, by Terry Southern and Mason Hoffenberg, p. 14)

7-14 Static type checking makes program execution both much faster and more reliable (since type errors are detected for all program paths during translation). *(Programming Languages: Design and Implementation*, 2nd ed., by Terrence W. Pratt, p. 224)

7-15 In the United States and in other developed countries, cigarette smoking has slid down the social scale from acceptable to somewhere between barely tolerable to reprehensible. Twenty-five years ago more than 50 percent of our adults smoked; today only about 32 percent do. ("Let's Stop Exporting the Smoking Epidemic," by Walter S. Ross, *Reader's Digest*, May 1980, p. 143)

7-16 I figure it's worth keeping so it's worth genuine GM Parts. And genuine Mr. Goodwrench good service. (Ad for GM, *Changing Times*, February 1982, pp. 40-41)

7-17 Producing varied and distinctive kinds of candy depends entirely on arriving at certain established stages of crystallization; and crystallization, in turn, depends on temperature. For this reason an accurate professional candy thermometer, properly used, is invaluable. ("About Candy Thermometer Temperatures," *Joy of Cooking*, by Irma S. Rombauer and Marion Rombauer Becker, p. 777)

7-18 Who says small children can't be included in challenging backpacking adventures? Not I. Our one 4-year-old and two 6-year-olds hiked 500 miles across the hills of western Nepal, even carrying their own backpacks. ("Trekking with Kids Through Nepal," by Ginny Moore, *Sierra*, November/December 1982, p. 43)

7-19 Those who deal in stolen car parts are unlikely to be apprehended because the only parts marked with identification numbers are the engine and transmission. It is practically impossible to trace unmarked parts. ("To Catch a Thief," *Motorist*, November/December 1983, p. 3)

7-20 The census, say political observers, also helps to explain why Congress is afraid of reducing Social Security benefits. Three-quarters of 63- and 64-year-old Americans turned up to vote, compared with only one-third of 18- and 19-year-olds. ("The Lie That Millions Tell About Voting," *Star*, June 29, 1982, p. 9)

7-21 A more important factor is the fear that patients will become addicted. Thus narcotics are given in doses that are often inadequate, at time intervals that are often too long, requiring the patient to wait out the time interval no matter how severe the pain. ("The Quality of Mercy" (from Marcia Angella, M.D., *New England Journal of Medicine*), "News from the World of Medicine," *Reader's Digest*, May 1982, p. 13)

7-22 Before you start many projects, it is a good idea to make a paper pattern for each of the parts of the project. A pattern will assist in marking and cutting the leather accurately, and you can also take it along when you shop for leather to assure getting enough with as few leftover scraps as necessary. (*Things to Make with Leather: Techniques & Projects*, p. 34)

7-23 The Sierra Club's membership stood at 350,119 on November 1, 1983. This represents an 86-percent increase since the Reagan administration began in January 1981; membership at that time was 188,740. ("Sierra Notes," *Sierra*, January/February 1984, p. 128)

7-24 The sodium levels in quiche vary widely. In Mrs. Smith's version, the salt and baking soda in the crust, and more salt, sodium propionate, sodium benzoate, cheese, and sometimes bacon in the filling, add up to 1,000 milligrams for each serving of pie. In contrast, Land O'Lakes' filling combined with Pillsbury or Betty Crocker's crust supply only about 400 mg per serving. ("Nouveau Rich: Trendy, New Food High in Fat," by Bonnie Liebman, *Nutrition Action*, January–February 1984, p. 12)

7-25 "They're going to feed you," said Roosta, "into the Total Perspective Vortex!"
   Zaphod had never heard of this. He believed that he had heard of all the fun things in the Galaxy, so he assumed that the Total Perspective Vortex was not fun. (*The Restaurant at the End of the Universe*, by Douglas Adams, p. 60)

Section 8

Unstated Premises and Conclusions; Extraneous Material

Introduction

The five argument structures introduced in the preceding two sections are the basic building blocks of all arguments. However, arguments may be complicated by not being presented very explicitly. These complications are illustrated by the examples of this section.

Unstated Premises

Sometimes an author will not state certain parts of her argument. Very often what is omitted is a premise of the argument. Premises are often left unstated because arguments are tailored to their audience: An author very often won't bother to state reasons that her audience already knows or views for which she is widely known. Consider the argument

> *Mr. Muldoon is the conservative Prime Minister of New Zealand, and Mr. Bennett a conservative Canadian politician; so, Muldoon and Bennett see eye to eye on a lot of political issues.*

If we were presenting this argument to a political audience in New Zealand, we might well not bother to state the premise about Muldoon, expecting that everyone in the audience would know these facts; but we would probably state the facts about Bennett because we could not be sure that people in the audience would know them. (The situation would, of course, be exactly reversed in presenting this argument in, say, a Canadian political newspaper.) Similarly, were Teddy Kennedy to argue that

> *Jerry Brown would be an excellent president—he has all the qualities of my late brother, Jack*

we would know that Teddy Kennedy believed J.F.K. to have had the qualities of an excellent president, and he would not have to state this as an explicit part of the argument.

Unstated Conclusions

Sometimes the missing part of the argument is the conclusion. The conclusion is usually left unstated only when it is fairly clear what the conclusion is. (Other times authors seem to not state their conclusion when they know that if it were stated, the weakness of their argument would be apparent; but they nonetheless hope the audience will draw that conclusion.) Arguments with unstated conclusions often seem to have more "punch"—it is almost as if when we are forced to draw the conclusion ourself, the conclusion has more chance of becoming firmly lodged in our brain. An example of an argument with an unstated conclusion is

> *In the 1980s, any presidential aspirant will have to curry favor amongst the Florida geriatric vote, and Senator Glenn certainly aspires to the presidency in the 1980s.*

At times, there can be both a missing premise and a missing conclusion. For example, if President Reagan argued

> *If Marxists took over the government of Canada, U.S. military assistance to liberate the Canadian people would be as justified as was similar assistance in Granada*

we would know that an unstated premise is Reagan's belief that the U.S. intervention in Granada was justified, and so we would know that the unstated conclusion of his argument is that U.S. military intervention in Canada under similar circumstances would be justified.

Obviously, if we are to present an author's complete argument when analyzing it, any unstated premises or conclusions must be explicitly stated. Unstated significant sentences in an argument should be written out under the passage, numbered, and enclosed in angle brackets. When the number of an unstated significant sentence is entered on an argument diagram, it should be placed in square brackets to indicate that it is unstated. For example, the above argument about Canada and Granada should be marked up and diagramed as follows:

< ① If Marxists took over the government of Canada, U.S. military assistance to liberate the Canadian people would be as justified as was similar assistance in Granada. >

< ② U.S. military assistance to liberate the Granadian people from their Marxist government was justified. >

< ③ U.S. military assistance to liberate the Canadian people from a Marxist government would be justified. >

$$\frac{① + [②]}{\big\downarrow}$$

$$[③]$$

We must exercise caution in adding unstated sentences. To be fair to the author of the argument, any added sentence should (a) not be a claim that you know the author would not accept, and (b) if possible, be a claim you know to be true. Still, where some claim is clearly essential to the argument and yet unstated, it should be added. Adding unstated parts to an argument may be of major assistance in assessing the argument, because occasionally it is the most questionable parts of the argument that somehow get left unstated.

Extraneous Material

Often we encounter the exact opposite of unstated parts of an argument—that is, excess verbiage that is not essential to the argument and can be trimmed from it. Sometimes this extraneous matter is simply fluff—words that pretty up the writing or make it dramatic. Other times it is more helpful. For instance, an author may state his conclusion more than once, perhaps before giving the argument for it and then after having given the argument. Usually, the conclusion won't be stated in exactly the same words both times. So although a repeat of the conclusion can be helpful, it is problematic if we misconstrue the restatement as a new significant sentence. Consider the following:

> *The voting population of California is schizoid—first they elect as governor a conservative old warhorse like Reagan, then they elect a leftie, young peacenik like Brown—those Californians have a split political personality.*

Clearly, the sentence before the first dash and after the second say virtually the same thing, though they use very different words. Both sentences can be angle bracketed and numbered with the same number. Extraneous matter that is simply fluff can be disregarded (which means it won't occur inside any set of angle brackets marked on the passage).

Although arguments are typically arguments for some conclusion, sometimes arguments are explicitly presented as reasons against a conclusion. Clearly, this calls for a little manipulation. Where the reasons given are all reasons *against* the stated conclusion, in analyzing the argument we can present the argument as reasons *for* the *negation* of the stated conclusion. This is not adequate where an argument considers both reasons for and reasons against the same conclusion. In such a case, reasons against can be diagrammed on the same diagram as the reasons for, but by using a squiggly arrow: 〰➤ . The straight arrow indicates that the sentence at its tail is a reason *for* the sentence at its head; the squiggly arrow indicates that the sentence at its tail is a reason *against* the sentence at its head. As an example consider the argument:

On balance (one has to conclude that) < ① probably no major third party will emerge on the American political scene this century. > (For) although < ② many voters are disillusioned with the two major parties, > < ③ previous attempts to build a major third party have always failed. >

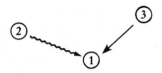

Given all the ways in which a passage may not clearly state the argument being presented, the reconstruction may often look quite unlike the original. This does not necessarily mean that the analysis is incorrect.

The following pointers may help in dealing with some less clear passages:

1. The references at the end of the passage may give vital information, such as the subject of the passage and the author of the argument. Because the references give the "environment" of the argument, they may help, for example, in formulating unstated parts of the argument.

2. Punctuation in the passage may give some clues about how to understand the passage, for example, in the absence of indicator words. Stronger punctuation more often separates premises from conclusion than the punctuation that separates one premise from another.

3. Everything that is angle bracketed and numbered should be a clear, complete sentence. If it is not, then it must be specified as a clear, complete sentence beneath the passage.

4. Extraneous verbiage and words that connect premises are not parts of any of the significant sentences of the argument; thus they should not occur inside any pair of angle brackets marked on the passage.

Two texts that have useful discussion of these issues are the following:

Jerry Cederblom and David W. Paulsen, *Critical Reasoning*, Ch. 3

Robert Baum, *Logic*, 2nd ed., pp. 91–95

Section 8: Instructions

Analyze the arguments in the passages that follow (if necessary, refer to the instructions in Sections 6 and 7 for the steps in giving an analysis).

Here is one example:

(Imaginary political campaign advertisement)

< ① Bogus Dissembler will lower your taxes. >

< ② You want lower taxes >

< ③ You should vote for Bogus Dissembler >

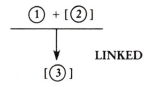

A second example is as follows:

It is exciting to realize that < ① American politics is slowly being liberated from the stranglehold of conventions that has gripped it for so long. > (First) , < ② a Catholic president >; (then) < ③ an ex-grade-B-actor president >. < ④ Recently an ex-astronaut candidate >; and < ⑤ a black candidate >. Can a woman candidate be far away? < ① No longer does one have to be WASP and a party hack to succeed in American politics. >

< ② A Catholic became the U.S. president >

< ③ An ex-grade-B actor became the U.S. president >

< ④ An ex-astronaut was recently a candidate for the U.S. presidency >

< ⑤ A black was recently a candidate for the U.S. presidency. >

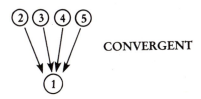

Section 8: Exercises

8-1 The most effective way I've found to save is to get up at 2 A.M. There are no afternoon shopping binges, no frivolous gifts for friends. It's draconian but it works. (Diane Sawyer, co-anchor of the CBS "Morning News," quoted in "True Confessions of Some Famous Savers," *Money,* August 1983, p. 69)

8-2 Sex can get better after 40, say two top psychologists. "Not only are you more experienced, you are also more familiar with your partner's needs, likes, and dislikes," says Dr. Eli Feldman of Great Neck, N.Y.

But, he adds, if your love life is to thrive, you have to give it all you have. And the fact is that you are better equipped to give it more as you get older. ("Ways You Can Make Your Love Life Better Than Ever After 40," *Star,* June 29, 1982, p. 46)

8-3 Advertising in the Bell System Yellow Pages means . . . business. (*Greater Birmingham Yellow Pages*, August 1982, p. 90)

8-4 The Senate Banking Committee is learning what taxpayers have known for some time—the U.S. Congress is a den of thieves.

Recently, the chairman's expensive hand-made gavel was stolen. A smaller, less expensive replacement was also taken. Then the lacquered plaque the chairman used to swear in witnesses vanished. A new plaque was ordered and chained to his desk—but one night plaque and chain both disappeared.

The chairman now reads the oath from photocopies. They get stolen too, but at least they are cheap. ("Life in the Senate Is a Crime," *Globe*, January 19, 1982, p. 11)

*8-5 The proper temperature in most instances is 365 degrees, as easy to remember as the number of days in the year. ("Deep-Fat Frying," *Joy of Cooking*, by Irma S. Rombauer and Marion Rombauer Becker, p. 147)

8-6 It is impossible to look through these old cookbooks without being struck by the quantity of dough which was crammed into the human system. Bread, rolls, biscuits, cakes and pastry are accorded the lion's share of their space. (*Eating in America: A History*, by Waverley Root and Richard de Rochemont, p. 136)

8-7 Q:

François Mitterand, president of France, enjoys the reputation of being a great Don Juan. I understand his limousine has been seen parked nightly outside the apartment of actress Dominique Sanda. What does Mme. Mitterand have to say about that little item?—E. F., Palm Beach, Fla.

A:

Danielle Mitterand, married to François since 1944, wisely has said nothing of gossip items about her husband. She is by nature a private and retiring person who does not equate the location of her husband's limousine with infidelity.

(Walter Scott's Personality Parade, *Parade*, January 10, 1982, p. 2)

8-8 The 1980 census spotlights one significant fact: Many Americans lied on their returns. Over 93 million people answered "yes" to the question, "Did you vote in the 1980 presidential election?" ("The Lie That Millions Tell About Voting," *Star*, June 29, 1982, p. 9)

8-9 Although Elvis consistently bought the friendship of his "Memphis Mafia" and the sexual favors of countless young women, he was, according to biographer Goldman, more the victim in life and afterlife than the victimizer. The IRS, for example, claims that the Presley estate owes more than $14 million in back taxes. ("Intelligence Report," by Lloyd Shearer, *Parade*, September 27, 1981, p. 8)

8-10   When reporters covering the Falklands-Malvinas crisis question the Buenos Aires man in the street for his views of the war, one of his often-quoted remarks is, "We are not 'Indians' "—meaning Argentines are made of superior stuff, and that the British will find out that Argentines are tough and hardy Europeans. After all, they defeated the British three times in the 19th century; they have won every war they have fought, including the 1976–79 campaign against Marxist guerrillas; they are even the world's foremost soccer and polo players. ("Blinkered Pride of the Arrogant Argentines," by Miguel Acoca, *Manchester Guardian Weekly*, June 13, 1982, p. 17)

8-11   Why is this pitcher smiling?

Because . . .

Kool-Aid Sugar-Sweetened is about ½ the price of soda.

Kool-Aid has Vitamin C. Soda doesn't.

Kool-Aid has no carbonation.

Kool-Aid Brand Soft Drink Mix has those big fruity flavors kids love.

   Hugs and Kisses guaranteed!

Make the smart choice.

Kool-Aid, instead of soda.

(Ad for Kool-Aid, *Reader's Digest*, May 1982, p. 201)

8–12 While alcohol is water soluble and washes out of the body, cannabinoids are fat soluble and accumulate in fatty sections of the cells and in fatty organs (the brain is one-third fat). ("Marijuana Alert III: The Devastation of Personality, " by Peggy Mann, *Reader's Digest*, December 1981, p. 83)

8–13 A whole-house fan (*Consumer Reports*, June 1981) would not be recommended for persons who have allergies to dust, molds, and pollens. The fan would blow the material around and aggravate the symptoms. A room air-conditioner with a good filter would be most helpful.—Maplewood, N.J. F.L.R., M.D. (Letter, *Consumer Reports*, September 1981, p. 545)

8–14 During the dinner, one of my guests commented on how exquisite the lace dinner napkins were. She examined the napkin carefully and fingered it admiringly. After my guest left, I was one napkin short! I searched all over, and finally came to the conclusion that the guest who had admired it must have taken it. (From a letter to Dear Abby, *Birmingham News*, September 4, 1982, p. 6C)

8-15 A solitary ant, afield, cannot be considered to have much of anything on his mind; indeed, with only a few neurons strung together by fibers, he can't be imagined to have a mind at all, much less a thought. (*The Lives of a Cell*, by Lewis Thomas, in "Points to Ponder," *Reader's Digest*, May 1982, p. 183)

8-16 Doesn't it make sense to own the Bell phone you lease . . . It's the best deal on a phone. Because it's right in your bedroom, den, living room, bathroom, hallway, basement or patio. (Bell Telephone ad, *Newsweek*, September 19, 1983, p. 35)

8-17 Risi e bisi is often listed on menus among the soups, and some gastronomic writers dare to call it one. Nonsense! It is served with a fork. Who ever heard of eating soup with a fork? ("Risi e bisi," *The Best of Italian Cooking*, by Waverley Root, p. 219)

8-18 Add naught to MacNaughton—because you don't dilute a great Canadian Whisky. (Billboard ad, I-20 southbound, Birmingham, Alabama, October 1983)

8-19 Your April 1981 report, "Good-bye, Leaded Premium Gasoline," stated that 15 million cars originally designed for leaded gasoline are on the road. But according to National Petroleum News Magazine, there are fewer than 5 million such cars—none of them built since 1972. Thus, the economics of supplying a special fuel to such a small and decreasing part of the market have become very unfavorable. It should come as no surprise that nearly all companies have dropped leaded premium gasoline. (Letter, *Consumer Reports*, August 1981, p. 432)

8-20 We still have the opportunity to save this area of unsurpassed splendor, but we must act now, for its natural, cultural, and scenic values are under siege at this very moment. ("It's Time to Save the Columbia River Gorge," by Senator Bob Packwood, *Sierra*, July/August 1983, p. 38)

8-21 There have been six serious incursions at the palace in the past year. In June 1981 three German tourists camped in the grounds under the impression that they were part of Hyde Park; in August a man was found in some bushes professing admiration for Princess Anne; in September a youth was arrested at the palace gates with an airgun; in December a mentally ill man was found in the grounds, and last month a man with an 8-inch dagger pushed past police into the gounds. ("Intruder Reaches Queen's Bedroom," by Martin Linton and Martin Wainwright, *Manchester Guardian Weekly*, July 18, 1982, p. 3)

8-22 Washington (AP)—For Robert Pond, fishing wouldn't be fishing without striped bass. So why is he trying to get the Maryland striper added to the endangered species list?

"The fish isn't reproducing because of pollution," said Pond . . . ("Maryland Striper May Soon Be Placed on Endangered List," *Birmingham News*, June 27, 1982, p. 14C)

8-23 Watch what happens when our soap meets water. It liquifies instantly. That's why Neutrogena washes off thoroughly. And you're left feeling immaculately clean, never dry or tight. (Ad for Neutrogena, *Reader's Digest*, May 1982, p. 207)

*8-24 Thousands of iron supplement pills made from freeze-dried seal liver were ordered withdrawn from the market; the pills, sold ironically in health food stores, contained up to 60 ppm of mercury. Said the president of the firm which made the pills, "Seal liver attracted my attention because it came from an animal most free of contaminants. You can just figure from this that there isn't any place in the whole earth that isn't contaminated." (*The Big, Fertile, Rumbling, Cast-Iron, Growling, Aching, Unbuttoned Belly-book*, by James Trager, pp. 305–306)

8-25 For a long time, the play keeps one guessing. We deduce that we are in an East European country (Yugoslavia?) that has endured German occupation, and that now enjoys a thriving tourist industry. ("Slow Burn," a review of Edward Bond's *Summer* at the Cottesloe, *Manchester Guardian Weekly*, February 14, 1982, p. 20)

*8-26 BE SEEN . . .
Advertise in the BELL SYSTEM YELLOW PAGES (*Greater Birmingham Yellow Pages*, August 1983, p. 719)

8-27 He did not pay much attention to the lecture. The physicist from the Weizmann Institute had been much more concise. "There is no such thing as a safe level of radiation," he had said. "Such talk makes you think that radiation is like water in a pool; if it's four feet high you're safe, it it's eight feet high you drown. But in fact radiation levels are much more like speed limits on the highway—thirty miles per hour is safer than eighty, but not as safe as twenty, and the only way to be completely safe is not to get in the car." (*Triple*, by Ken Follett, p. 71)

8-28 Trento, Italy—The gravedigger in the village of Cimego was "unemployed" last year and had to be given other duties to keep him busy.

Officials said that there were no deaths in 1981. Seven births swelled the population to 430. ("Gravedigger Gets No Work," *Birmingham Post-Herald*, January 6, 1982, p. E1)

*8-29 The frequent claim that no true scientist can be a Bible-believing Christian or creationist is refuted by the fact that the greatest scientists of earlier generations *did* believe the Bible and in God as Creator. ("Two New Books Published by ICR Scientists," *Acts & Facts*, March 1982, p. 2)

8-30 Since antiquity, meats have been salted to keep them from spoiling; but it took the advent of analytical chemistry to show that the red spots which sometimes developed in salted meats came from the nitrate impurities in the salt. Since people equate redness with freshness in meats, nitrites came to be used as color fixers to keep meat looking red and fresh when it was really an unappetizing gray or brown. (*The Big, Fertile, Rumbling, Cast-Iron, Growling, Aching, Unbuttoned Bellybook*, by James Trager, p. 355)

8–31 Question:

Why is it that in the past two weeks the price of eggs has soared from about 99 cents to $1.15 for a dozen of large eggs?

Answer one:

"When it gets cold, hens don't lay as much," says one local grocer.

("Egg Prices Are on Rise for a While," by Andrew Kilpatrick, *Birmingham News*, January 18, 1984, p. 1D)

8–32 Phoenix, Ariz.—The Roman Catholic Diocese of Phoenix has refused to marry a couple because the man is a quadriplegic unable to consummate the union, the church says. . . . He retains some use of his arms and hands, but is paralyzed from the chest down. ("Church Refuses to Marry Couple," *Birmingham Post-Herald*, July 5, 1982, p. C10)

8–33 He [Sartre] did not write like a philosopher either, for he commanded a graceful prose style that could turn the subtlest concept into a memorable aphorism or a playable drama. ("Inadvertent Guru to an Age," *Time*, April 28, 1980, p. 39)

8-34 After all, how do you know that I am conscious? Obviously because I tell you so, and because I am built rather like you, and you are therefore happy to extrapolate from knowledge of your own conscious experience and accept that I too share this attribute. (*Seeing: Illusion, Brain and Mind*, by John P. Frisby, p. 158)

8-35 Other discoveries were also made, and one of the most significant appears in the accompanying photograph, which shows a strange cloud of dust billowing up from the surface of Io, one of the moons of Jupiter. At first thought to be the debris thrown up by an impacting meteor, further computer enhancement and analysis showed that it was in fact the result of a volcanic eruption. Jupiter, then, has at least one moon which is still geologically active. ("Update on Space Exploration," *Theorist*, Fall 1983, p. 1)

8-36 The evidence for evolution on the continental shelf is even more dramatic. Areas far from shore teem with many and diverse species, which arise there more frequently than they do nearer the shore. For that reason, "one would think that this is where novelties come from," says paleontologist David Jablonski of the University of Arizona. ("Evolution in Hard Places," by Sharon Begley, *Newsweek*, January 2, 1984, p. 60)

8-37 The meeting again discouraged an enthusiast. A young woman, quite beautiful but disorderly, and clearly crazed by altruism, said that she could take at least twenty refugees into her home.

Somebody else got up and said to her that she was such an incompetent housekeeper that her own children had gone to live with other relatives.

Another person pointed out to her that she was so absent-minded that her dog would have starved to death, if it weren't for neighbors, and that she had accidentally set fire to her house three times. (*Slapstick, or Lonesome No More!* by Kurt Vonnegut, p. 217)

8-38 Why is competition among scientists so keen for the 280-odd berths underwritten by the National Scientific Foundation in Antarctica? A key reason, many of them say, is that Antarctica has actually become a kind of space station—a unique observation post for detecting important changes in the world's environment. Remote from major sources of pollution and the complex geological and ecological systems that prevail elsewhere, Antarctica makes possible scientific measurements that are often sharper and easier to interpret than those made in other parts of the world. ("Antarctica: Earth's Early-Warning Station," by Malcolm W. Browne, *Discover*, February 1984, p. 91)

8-39 When asked whether an organic computer is feasible, Louis Robinson, IMB's director of university relations, replies: "In science it's foolish to say something is impossible." ("Silicon's Successor? Tomorrow's Computer May Reproduce Itself, Some Visionaries Think," by Susan Chace, *Wall Street Journal*, January 6, 1983, p. 12)

8-40   Late Sunday, when they [Cody and Luke] returned, Ruth came out to the driveway. The night was chilly, and she wore no sweater but hugged herself as she walked towards the car, her white, freckled face oddly set and her faded red hair standing up in the wind. That was how Cody guessed something was wrong. Ruth hated cold weather, and ordinarily would have waited inside the house. (*Dinner at the Homesick Restaurant*, by Anne Tyler, p. 285)

Section 9

Complex Arguments

Introduction

Just as many houses of very different design can be constructed from one type of brick, so the five basic argument structures allow the construction of arguments of many different overall "shapes." The examples of this section illustrate the further complexity in analyzing arguments built from the five basic structures.

There is no limit, in theory, to the complexity an argument may have; however, as arguments increase in complexity, they become more and more difficult to express clearly in English. (In contrast, an argument of any level of complexity can be clearly and unambiguously expressed in an argument diagram.) Often complexity is something that gets gradually built into an argument as it is refined. For example, imagine that we start out with an argument that is convergent with three reasons:

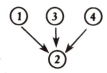

However, on looking over the first draft of the argument, we see that reason ④ will probably not be accepted by our audience without some evidence. On consideration we realize that our reason for ④ is, in fact, a serial argument, which gives the structure

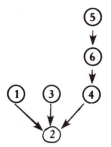

Now we realize that ② is not quite the conclusion we intended to argue for. However, the conclusion we intended follows from ② and another premise that we do not need to state because it is well known to our audience. So the structure now is

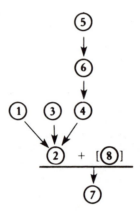

But having thought through the argument from ② + ⑧ to ⑦ , we realize that ⑦ is not the only conclusion that follows from ② + ⑧ — and we decide to explicitly state the further conclusion. Thus the final structure is

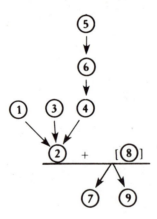

This is a complex argument, but it is built up out of components that come from the five basic argument structures.

Here is another example—this time in English, with the English passage marked up and an argument diagram given:

< ① *Cross-country skiing will continue to gain in popularity in the USA* > *(because)* < *②it's a very healthy form of exercise* > *and*

< ③ *Americans will turn more and more to winter sports in the future*>

< ② *Cross-country skiing is a very healthy form of exercise*>

But ② is a reason for ① only on the assumption that Americans are increasingly taking up healthy forms of exercise, and as that assumption may not be shared by our audience, we decide to state it explicitly:

< ① *Cross-country skiing will continue to gain in popularity in the USA*> (*because*) < ② *it's a very healthy form of exercise*>, and < ④ *Americans are increasingly taking up healthy forms of exercise*>; *and, moreover*, < ③ *Americans will turn more and more in the future to winter sports*>

Notice the changes: the introduction of the heavier punctuation (the semi-colon at the end of ④) and the addition of 'moreover' to indicate that ② and ④ go together, whereas ③ is separate from them. Now we decide to add our reasons for ③ , which are

< ③ *Americans will turn more and more to winter sports in the future*>, (*because*) < ⑤ *atmospheric pollution will continue to increase*> (*which suggests*) *that* < ⑥ *the Earth will get cooler*> *and* (*so*) < ⑦ *winters will get longer*>

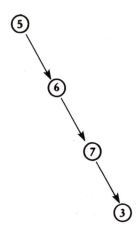

Realizing that putting all this together is going to give us a passage that will be difficult to read, we decide to put in some more explicit inference indicators:

(There are two main reasons for thinking that) < ① *cross-country skiing will continue to gain in popularity in the USA* >: *(first)*, < ② *it's a very healthy form of exercise* >, *and* < ④ *Americans are increasingly taking up healthy forms of exercise* >; *(second)*, < ③ *Americans will turn more and more to winter sports in the future* >, *(because)* < ⑤ *atmospheric pollution will continue to increase* > *(which suggest that)* < ⑥ *the Earth will get cooler* > *and so* < ⑦ *winters will get longer* >

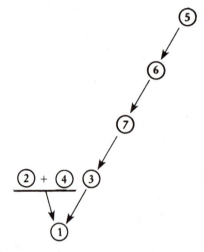

These two examples show how we might be led to construct a complex argument. The other side of the coin is, of course, analyzing a complex argument that someone else has constructed.

There is no set way in which we should go about analyzing a complex argument, but the earlier we can determine the general overall structure of the argument, the easier the process becomes. First, we should identify the inference indicators and then attempt to determine the overall conclusion in the passage (and perhaps the basic reasons that are stated but for which no arguments are given). Once the general overall structure is clear, the detailed subarguments within that structure will be easy to analyze.

Consider this example:

St. Joe, Florida, has no local professional sports team but despite that, when you weigh the opposing considerations, it seems that a professional ice-hockey team in town would not succeed. To build and operate an ice-hockey stadium in St. Joe would be very expensive because of the temperatures involved, and so a team would have to charge a lot for tickets. Moreover, because ice skating is virtually unknown to the locals, there is no local enthusiasm for this sport; and where tickets cost a lot and there is no local enthusiasm for the sport, a professional team cannot survive.

From the way the first sentence ends it seems as if this, overall, is an argument for the conclusion that a professional ice hockey team in St. Joe would not succeed, though the sentence actually begins with a consideration in favor of the opposite conclusion. The second sentence establishes that such a team would have to charge a lot for tickets; the third sentence up to the semicolon establishes that there is no local enthusiasm for the sport; and the fragment after the semicolon claims that where these two conditions hold, a team cannot succeed. These three claims seem to be the reasons in a linked argument for the overall conclusion, and so the overall structure of most of the passage is that of a linked argument. 'So' and 'because' in the second sentence indicate there is an argument structure here and it seems to be serial—something about temperatures is a reason for the claim that a stadium would be expensive, which in turn is a reason for saying that tickets would be costly. In the third sentence up to the semicolon, there is only one inference indicator, which suggests a simple argument from a fact about ice skating to a claim about local enthusiasm for ice hockey. The argument can be analyzed as follows:

< ① *St. Joe, Florida, has no local professional sports team*> *but despite that, when you weigh the opposing considerations, it seems that* < ② *a professional ice-hockey team in town would not succeed*>. < ③ *To build and operate an ice-hockey stadium in St. Joe would be very expensive*> (*because of*) < ④ *the temperatures involved*>, *and* (*so*) < ⑤ *a team would have to charge a lot for tickets*>. *Moreover,* (*because*) < ⑥ *ice skating is virtually unknown to the locals*>, < ⑦ *there is no local enthusiasm for this sport*>; *and* < ⑧ *where tickets cost a lot and there is no local enthusiasm for the sport, a professional team cannot survive*>.

< ② *A professional ice-hockey team in St. Joe would not succeed*> < ④ *St. Joe has a warm climate and an ice-hockey stadium needs cold temperatures*> < ⑤ *A professional ice-hockey team in St. Joe would have to charge a lot for tickets*> < ⑥ *Ice skating is virtually unknown to the locals of St. Joe*> < ⑦ *There is no local enthusiasm for ice hockey in St. Joe*>

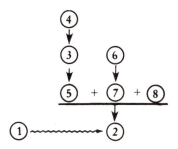

The analysis of complex arguments is discussed in

> Stephen N. Thomas, *Practical Reasoning in Natural Language*,
> 2nd ed., Ch. 1–4

Techniques for handling extended passages, which could be used with the techniques described here, are explained in

> Howard Kahane, *Logic and Contemporary Rhetoric*, 4th ed., Ch. 6

Section 9: Instructions

Analyze the arguments in the passages that follow (if necessary, refer to the instructions in Sections 6 and 7 for the steps in giving an analysis. For example:

Backpacking will never become an Olympic sport for, while it is certainly possible to judge one backpacker to be better than another, the standards of excellence in backpacking are too subjective and vague for precise discriminations to be made. Thus the makers of backpacking equipment will never be able to use the Olympics to advertise their products.

This passage is marked to yield

< ①︎ **Backpacking will never become an Olympic sport** > (for), while < ②︎ **it is certainly possible to judge one backpacker to be better than another** >, < ③︎ **the standards of excellence in backpacking are too subjective and vague for precise discriminations to be made** >. (Thus) < ④︎ **the makers of backpacking equipment will never be able to use the Olympics to advertise their products** >.

An unstated premise needs to be added:

< ⑤︎ **To be an Olympic sport, the standards of excellence in that sport must be objective and not vague** >

and an argument diagram given:

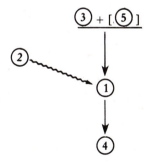

Section 9: Exercises

9-1 Refining grains to make white flour lowers the usable protein because much of the lysine, already in short supply in grains, is lost when the germ is removed from the grain. Thus, products made with whole wheat provide more protein than those prepared from refined white flour. (*Jane Brody's Nutrition Book*, by Jane E. Brody, pp. 52–53)

9-2 Why has the Japanese auto industry succeeded in taking over 22% of the American market? Basic reason: it costs the Japanese about $1500 less than it cost Detroit to manufacture a comparable vehicle.

According to "Business Week," the Japanese worker is paid $10 an hour in wages and benefits to do what the American worker is supposed to do for $18.50 an hour.

Moreover, it takes twice as many executives and laborers to produce a car here.

In short, we are top-heavy in wages and manpower. ("The Reason Why," Parade's Special Intelligence Report, by Lloyd Shearer, *Parade*, December 20, 1981, p. 9)

9-3 A roaring bonfire was once considered an essential part of being outdoors. How chummy it was to sit around the evening campfire, singing songs and toasting marshmallows. But today the wilderness can't support many campfires. Living trees are a precious resource, and dead wood is part of the natural landscape. Cooking can be done more quickly and efficiently over a backpacking stove than over an open fire anyway, so why not use a stove and preserve the landscape? Save the marshmallows for home or for established campsites. (*Backpacking*, by Michael Sandi, p. 34)

9-4   Q: President Reagan gave only seven press conferences in his first year in office. President Jimmy Carter held 23 in his first year. Why has Reagan given so few?—L.T., Sherman Oaks, Cal.

A: Reagan is a superb speechmaker when using a prepared script or outline. In a question-and-answer press conference, however, where he is required to respond extemporaneously, he occasionally "misspeaks." In his White House press conference of Jan.19, 1982, for example, Reagan "misspoke" on several subjects, including employment rates, civil rights, the California abortion statute and national security disclosures. While most recent Presidents preferred to air their press conferences on prime TV time, Reagan has scheduled his for 2 P.M. or 4 P.M., reducing his audience by half.

("Walter Scott's Personality Parade," *Parade,* March 14, 1982, p.2)

9-5   Make it easy on yourself. Mail your telephone payment every month, and let the mailman do the walking—or the driving.

When you pay by mail, you also help us keep expenses down. It's cheaper for us to process payments received by mail. And that helps keep down the price of your service.

MAIL IT! (South Central's Bell Notes, November 1982)

9–6 With the demise of the ancient Caledonian forests of birch and pine, so the deer became increasingly deprived of shelter so that more of their reserves of energy had to be devoted to keeping warm and adequately nourished so that their physical stature progressively declined. ("Stag Party," by Veronica Heath, *Manchester Guardian Weekly,* October 23, 1983, p. 19)

9–7 While Alabama Power and South Central Bell attracted the headlines and hate mail over rate increases during the past five years, gas rates rose more sharply than charges from either of the two higher-profile utilities.

Alabama Gas Corporation in 1977 billed an average residential gas user $204.17, at January prices, for a year's worth of natural gas, said spokesman Jim Alderman.

That same amount of gas—937 ccf (hundred cubic feet)—cost $486.45 this month, a 238 percent increase over 1977.

Local residential phone service went up 21 percent during the same period, from $12.25 a month in 1977 to $14.80 a month in 1981, said Bell spokesman Walter Sechriest.

Alabama Power Company upped its charge per kilowatt hour of electricity 46 percent, from 3.85 cents in 1977 to 5.62 cents in 1981, said APC spokesman Ed Crosby. ("You Think Electricity, Phone Rates Rising? Take Look at Gas Bill," by Dave White, *Birmingham News,* January 31, 1982, p.1. Reprinted by permission)

9-8 Ironically, though hunt supporters referred to "opening" the [Loxahatchee National Wildlife] refuge, the hunt in fact temporarily closed the southern end to some regular recreational activities. Fishing and boating were curbed to protect the public. Canoeing along the Everglades canoe trail was halted because the hunt site was too close. ("Defenders' Suit Cuts Loxahatchee Hunt by Two-thirds; Two Deer Shot," *Defenders*, January/February 1984, p. 42)

9-9 Everybody talks about quality. Ford people make it happen. Take our attention to craftsmanship, for example. There are still some things that the human hand can do better than a machine, like the final polishing of a die. A detail which can take from 40 to 120 work hours, and is done so that the sheet metal in doors and body panels is not blemished during the stamping process.

Visit a Ford or Lincoln-Mercury dealer and take a close look at what total employee, management, union and supplier involvement can achieve. (Ad for Ford automobiles, *Reader's Digest*, May 1982, p. 9)

9-10 When buying sunglasses for utility and not just for their looks, choose either neutral gray or sage green lenses. These give you good color perception with very little distortion, and both provide excellent protection from the glare of sunlight. (*Field and Stream*, July 1981, p. 112)

*9-11 Contrary to the public image of dinosaurs as the Edsels of evolution, says Colbert, they were extraordinarily well-adapted creatures. They inhabited every corner of the world and ranged in bulk from the chicken-sized Compsognathus to the 100-ton Brachiosaurus, the largest creature ever to tread the earth. Though they plodded through swamps and shallow coastal waters, they were essentially land bound. Some ambled on all fours; others scampered after prey on their lower limbs. Some may have lived a century or more. ("Debunking Dinosaur Myths," *Time*, October 17, 1983, p. 57)

9-12 [Laurence] Sterne [author of *Tristram Shandy*], who occasionally preached in the York Minster, died and first was buried in London. "Gravediggers, not knowing who he was, took his body to Cambridge where it was used for an anatomy lecture. Sterne was recognized, though, and his body returned to London," Monkham said. "In 1969 the burial ground was sold for development. So, Sterne was up for reburial. I went down and spotted a skeleton whose skull had been sawed in half. It was obviously as far as the anatomy professor had gotten. But to confirm it was really Sterne, I hurried home to measure Nolleken's bust of him. The sculpted head and the skull were exactly the same, including a protrusion which accounted for Sterne's slightly bucked teeth." ("City of Mystery," by Landt Dennis, *Saturday Review*, August 1983, p. 23)

*9-13 Unwrap your fragrant soap and place it in dresser drawers to impart its aroma to your belongings. The soap will harden, unwrapped, and last much longer when you do start to use it. ("No. 1 Defense Against Colds: Wash Hands," by Dorsey Connors, *Birmingham News*, January 27, 1982, p. 6E)

9-14   The rationales for saving wild species, at the onset of the movement several decades ago, were largely ethical, esthetic, and ecological. These fundamental arguments have since been joined by another, equally important one. We depend on our fellow species for our material welfare, and ultimately for our future survival, in all sorts of unspecified ways. ("By Saving Wild Species, We May Be Saving Ourselves," by Norman Myers, *Nature Conservancy News*, November/December 1983, p. 7)

9-15   There is something else about women that every man should know—probably the single most important thing.—*Women are good for him.*
       The happiest people in the world are married men; the unhappiest are bachelors. And married men live longer. A recent study found that widowers between the ages of 45 and 64 had a 61 percent higher mortality rate than married men in the same age bracket. But widowers need not despair. The mortality rate for those who remarry was no higher than that for married men in general. ("What Men Should Know About Women," by Dr. Joyce Brothers, *Parade*, January 3, 1982, p. 5)

9-16   Artificial intelligence is not the study of computers. Computers are metallic machines of intrinsic interest to electronic engineers but not, as such, to many others. So if you are not enamored of tin cans, you need not fear to meet any in this book. (*Artificial Intelligence and Natural Man* by Margaret A. Boden, p. 4)

9-17 VIOLENT BOYFRIEND

Dear Meg: I want to end things with my guy. Stan's sweet, but I don't love him. There's no way I can just end the relationship, for several reasons. First of all, I'm scared. He has beaten me up a few times because I had it coming to me.

Meg, it would destroy him if I just walked out. He says he has nothing to live for but me. He has five children but none ever visits or calls him. How can I end this relationship without causing a commotion?—Mary Ann, Princeton, N.J. (*Star*, June 29,1982, p. 40)

9-18 If you are a musician who's serious about performing, you should take a serious look at the Army.

Army bands offer you an average of 40 performances a month. In everything from concerts to parades.

Army bands also offer you a chance to travel.

The Army has bands performing in Japan, Hawaii, Europe and all across America.

And Army bands offer you the chance to play with good musicians. Just to qualify you have to be able to sightread music you've never seen before and demonstrate several other musical skills. (Army recruitment ad, *Rolling Stone*, September 16, 1982, p. 84)

9-19 Besides being a very natural and readable way to convert various levels of an algorithm into code, procedures serve several other useful purposes. They permit us to isolate repetitive sections of code into one location and in so doing are a great labor-saving device. Further, if they are general and independent, we can now remove these sections of code and transport them from program to program. Thus useful sections of code which we might use again and again should probably be written as procedures (mean, standard deviation, and sorting routines are examples).

The other big advantage to procedures is that they make for "clean" code in the main procedure. . . . Someone reading such code is not distracted from the main procedure by the detailed code . . . yet it is there should he be interested. (*Problem Solving and the Computer: A Structured Concept with PL/I (Pl/C)*, 2nd ed., by Joseph Short and Thomas C. Wilson, pp. 240-241)

9-20 WITH SUGAR PUFFS HE'LL EAT UP THE CEREAL, NOT THE BUDGET

With today's high cereal prices, the trick is finding a cereal your kids will like, at a price that won't strain the budget.

The solution is Sugar Puffs—sweetened puffs of wheat, packed with nutrition and a delicious flavor that kids love. Yet they cost about 35 cents less than the leading boxed brands.

Try Sugar Puffs cereal in the bag. (Ad for Sugar Puffs, *Family Circle*, July 20, 1982, p. 19)

9-21 There is also increasing unease about the ecological impact of the eucalyptus. Permitting no undergrowth, eucalyptus contributes little to the build-up of humus and is known to be a voracious consumer of water. The Bangalore report concludes: "The long-term impact of eucalyptus on the fertility of agricultural land is expected to be deleterious." ("Indian Forests up a Gum Tree," by Nicholas Hildyard, *Manchester Guardian Weekly*, July 3, 1983, p. 8)

9-22 Tax laws also have helped to encourage borrowing. When you borrow, the interest you pay on the loan is tax deductible. But when you lend, the interest you receive is taxable. So there are more borrowers and fewer lenders, with the result that interest rates have climbed. ("Do You Own Too Much?" by John R. Dorfman, *Parade*, December 5, 1982 p. 18)

9-23 Grandmother disapproved of candy, not because of tooth decay or indigestion, but because children liked it and children should perforce not have anything they liked. ("R Is for Romantic," *An Alphabet for Gourmets*, in *The Art of Eating*, by M. F. K. Fisher, p. 679)

9-24 Fall is the best time to visit America's great cities, beaches and mountains. The foliage is breathtaking, the weather is cooler and the crowds are gone. So you can really relax and enjoy yourself. (Ad for Amtrak, *Parade*, November 13, 1983, p. 22)

*9-25 "There are a lot of 'dryer only' purchases because a dryer usually lasts longer than a washer," said Joy Schrage, manager of communications for Whirlpool Corp. in Benton Harbor, Mich.

"An automatic washer lasts an average of 11 years. A gas dryer lasts about 13 years. And an electric dryer lasts about 15 years." ("A Month for Dryers," by Judy Moore, *Birmingham News*, September 23, 1981, p. 1G)

9-26 What emerges with great clarity from the book is that Jung has done immense service both to psychology as a science and to our general understanding of man in society, by insisting that imaginative life must be taken seriously, in its own right, as the most distinctive characteristic of human beings. (Blurb on back cover of *Man and His Symbols*, by Carl G. Jung et al.)

9-27 No nonsense about noise: we all should keep a pair of earplugs handy, says communication specialist Lillian H. Glass, Ph.D., University of Southern California School of Medicine. Dr. Glass believes earplugs ought to be more common as personal accessories than sunglasses, because overexposure to noise is more common than overexposure to the sun's glare. "Noise not only threatens one of your senses," says Dr. Glass, "but it endangers your general health and sanity." She adds that research links excessive noise to insomnia, ulcers, high blood pressure, and heart disease. ("Bad Noise News," Health, by Melva Weber, *Vogue*, Fall 1981, p. 91)

9-28 I'm 15 1/2. Many people tell me that I'm real nice and pretty, but no one ever asks me out.

The guys my age don't ask me because I am very mature and look much older than my age.

The older guys don't ask me out because they know my true age and all their friends would tease them about going out with a younger girl. . . . — Discouraged ("'Pretty' Girl Not Getting Any Dates," in "What's Your Hangup? A Guide for Teens," by Jean Adams, *Birmingham News*, January 14, 1982, p. 11D)

9-29 No matter how tough your kids are on shoes, they still aren't too tough for Hush Puppies children's shoes.

We made them tough and sturdy. And Breathin' Brushed Pigskin leather makes them rain and stain resistant, plus easy to clean. Now that's a whole lot of shoe for your money.

Kids love the way they look and feel. So comfortable and flexible.

Go for the value of Hush Puppies children's shoes and feel confident that your little ones will get a lot out of them. And they're priced just right, too. (Ad for Hush Puppies children's shoes, *Good Housekeeping*, September 1983, p. 247)

9-30 N. Michael Niflis: Teaching is something that takes place *only* when learning does. No matter what the teacher is doing in his classes, if his students are not learning something *significant* he is not teaching. When the student fails, the teacher has failed more. ("Points to Ponder," *Reader's Digest,* May 1982, p. 183)

9-31 In other words, in microphysics the observer interferes with the experiment in a way that can't be measured and that therefore can't be eliminated. No natural laws can be formulated, saying "such-and-such will happen in every case." All the microphysicist can say is "such-and-such is, according to statistical probability, likely to happen." . . . It could thus be said that scientists can no longer hope to describe any aspects or qualities of outer objects in a completely independent, "objective" manner. ("Science and the Unconscious," by M. L. Franz, *Man and His Symbols,* by Carl G. Jung et al., p. 382)

9–32 I'd much rather be remembered for what I'm doing now—and there are reasons for that: you always want to be identified if possible with your more recent work, because that is what I'm doing now not what I did yesteryear; and, I want to feel that I've grown. (Composer Richard Adler, interviewed by Bob Edwards on "Morning Edition," NPR, WUAL, December 28, 1983)

9–33 The warranty covers only major structural defects.

HOW defines a "major structural defect" as actual damage to a load-bearing component of the house. . . . In a house with a trussed-roof system, all the load is carried by the outside walls, so no inside wall would be considered load-bearing; no cracks in such a wall would be covered. ("Housing Yourself in the 80's: How Good Are Home Warranties?" *Consumer Reports*, July 1981, p. 407)

9–34 EVERYTIME YOU SCRATCH YOUR HEAD, YOU COULD BE TELLING SOMEONE YOU HAVE DANDRUFF.

Because a dry, itchy scalp can mean dandruff. And, recent studies show most people still have some.

So take care of that itch with Head & Shoulders. It controls the cause of dandruff, and leaves the hair soft, shiny, and manageable.

Then all you'll be likely to tell people is how you got such great-looking hair. (Ad for Head & Shoulders shampoo, *Cosmopolitan*, October 1979, p. 361)

*9-35 The computer increasingly lets knowledge be something that can immediately be used, rather than something that must be simply learned for an exam. Another important benefit of using the computer as a tool for discovery is that most students find it fun to play with computers, trying out their ideas for new programs and so students can get enjoyably involved in their work. (*Computers and the Cybernetic Society*, by Michael A. Arbib, p. 333)

9-36 I believe you'll be happy with GEICO. You'll certainly like our low rates guaranteed for one full year. Plus, you'll appreciate our convenient payment plans . . . countrywide claim service . . . and the security of insuring your car with a company that has over 40 years of experience.

   All good reasons why you should send us your application today. (From an advertising letter from GEICO, June 1982)

9-37 Dear Dr. Graham: My husband is convinced that Jesus Christ is coming again very soon. He is so convinced of this that he refuses to get a job or support our family because we need to be prepared for Christ's coming. ("My Answer," *Birmingham News*, June 28, 1982, p. 5C)

9-38 Why are you still using soap when women from Scranton to Sacramento will tell you Dove is better? There is no question about it.

Dove is better for your face than soap. . . . You see, soap dries your skin.

It strips away your skin's natural moisturizer. It cleans your face—*dry*.

But Dove is not soap.

It's made quite differently with 1/4 moisturizing cream.

So it keeps your skin softer, smoother.

Try Dove instead of soap for just 7 days and prove it for yourself:

Dove is better because it doesn't dry like soap. (Ad for Dove soap, *Family Circle*, September 1982, p. 37)

9-39 So, if you think you would like to lead a Sierra Club outing right now, or perhaps lead one next year, I would encourage you to complete the registration form below and return it as soon as possible.

There are several reasons why I make that statement. One is that the leadership seminar is held when the fall colors are showing. Another is that this time of year is Oktoberfest in Helen. A third is that we have a brand new leaders' guide available with the "where to hike in north Georgia" resource included for new outings leaders. Also, at this time of the year it is warm during the day, but there's a nice crisp coolness to the air in the evening. Finally, because these seminars have been so well attended in the past, we will have to put a limit on the number of participants. ("Ever Wanted to Lead a Hike? Here's a Chance to Learn How!" by Paul Weekley, *Chattahoochee Sierran*, September 1982, p. 3)

9-40 But as an agency without enforcement powers, the IWC can do nothing when member nations exceed kill quotas, hunt in proscribed waters or otherwise operate outside regulations. It has had to stand by helplessly while "pirate" whalers slaughtered protected species, pregnant females and young— and sold the meat to Japanese whale importers. While whale populations were declining in the world's oceans, the IWC too often has ignored the recommendations of its own scientists and has rubber-stamped the swollen quotas demanded by whaling interests. ("Let the Great Whales Live!" by Andrew Jones, *Reader's Digest*, May 1982, p. 170)

9-41 Trying to predict the future of the economy is always risky, but there seems to be one safe bet: It's going to be increasingly dominated by computers.

And that could spell trouble for women.

The ability to master the computerized office or business of tomorrow will be essential for the success of managers. But a growing number of experts are concerned that females may be unwittingly limiting their career potentials by shying away from computers.

This tendency is evident from kindergarten on up to the college level. While girls do about as well as boys on computer literacy tests, and while more and more women are majoring in computer science, most of them shun the extracurricular activities that could give them an edge.

A number of reasons are offered. They include parental bias, which discourages girls from studying math; video-game violence, which turns girls off, and male-oriented computer advertising. ("Computers—For Boys Only?" *Birmingham Post-Herald*, July 3, 1982, p. A4. Reprinted by permission)

9–42 FLEXIBLE HIGHWAYS

Rubber from millions of worn-out tires may once again be part of the automotive transportation scene, but this time in the road rather than on it. Tests carried out in Alaska have shown that asphalt containing 3 to 4 percent of rubber particles two to six millimeters in size has several advantages over other paving materials. These include better traction, lower noise levels, and enhanced ability to shed wintertime ice. In addition, rubberized roads appear to be more resistant to fatigue and cracking.

Apparently, the flexing of the exposed rubber particles in the pavement under the passing vehicles causes ice to break into small pieces rather than stick to the surface in sheets. According to David C. Esch, chief of highway research for the Alaska Department of Transportation and Public Facilities, savings in the cost of ice control alone could justify the expense of adding rubber to the pavement mix. The technique could be particularly useful where the sand and salt used for ice control are costly to apply and have undesirable environmental effects. ("Innovations," ed. Harold A. Rodgers, *Technology Illustrated*, June/July 1982, p. 18. Reprinted by permission)

9–43 O'Neill seems out of place in the luxury of those rooms [his "private" office]. He . . . appears rumpled and somewhat untidy, like someone unaware of what he's wearing . . .

He has five children. By normal Congressional standards, he is a poor man. He lives on his salary. ("Tip O'Neill: He Needs a Win," by Dotson Rader, *Parade*, September 27, 1981, p. 4)

9-44 Before the embargo, nations in Eastern Europe had ordered 16 million tons of American grains. When the embargo began, they suddenly increased their orders to more than 18 million tons, and the grain was sold to them without delay. "You'd have to be pretty naive to believe that increased exports to that area would not find their way to Russia," said the president of the Saskatchewan Wheat Pool in Canada in Spring 1980. ("Food: America's Secret Weapon," by Lowell Ponte, *Reader's Digest*, May 1982, p. 66)

9-45 Colder bedrooms aren't the only reason for the popularity of comforters. At about the same time that people were looking for warmer bedding, sheet manufacturers were looking for ways to increase the market for their products. Clothing designers were called in to give sheets a fashion flair, and sheets became too pretty to be hidden under a bedspread. Why not make a comforter to match the sheeting and do away with the bedspread altogether? Newly developed comforters could be more affordable. ("Comforters," *Consumer Reports*, January 1984, p. 23)

9-46 It is an important and popular fact that things are not always what they seem. For instance, on the planet Earth, man has always assumed that he was more intelligent than dolphins because he had achieved so much—the wheel, New York, wars, and so on—while all the dolphins had ever done was muck about in the water having a good time. But conversely, the dolphins had always believed that they were far more intelligent than man—for precisely the same reasons. (*The Hitchhiker's Guide to the Galaxy*, by Douglas Adams, p. 156)

9–47 In his work, the cleric also was called upon to exorcise spirits from dwellings. "They ranged all the way from public housing to old inns to old houses," he recalls.

"These are not difficult to drive out. Prayer and blessing the premises usually does the trick. I've rarely been called to the same place twice, and if I don't get called back I assume the work is done. ("Demons Taking Over Says Top Exorcist," *Globe*, August 16, 1983, p. 2)

9–48 You say that "Vega is visible only in the Northern Hemisphere." The declination, or angle above the celestial equator, of Vega, is 38 degrees north. Thus, anyone living north of latitude 52 degrees south, which includes most of the Southern Hemisphere as well as the entire Northern Hemisphere, can observe this star at some time during the year.—Amiel Sternberg, New York, N.Y. ("Letters," *Newsweek*, September 19, 1983, p. 9)

9–49 Why study language development in chimpanzees? Wouldn't it be better to study how language develops in the child?

Dr. Rumbaugh:
Chimpanzees learn language much more slowly than people and require special tutoring. So, with chimps we can get a better perspective as to both the factors that facilitate the learning and the factors that interfere with the learning. Also, with apes we can exercise great control. For example, we can completely control their training. We can make the chimps proficient in some areas of language but not in others; we can systematically emphasize certain aspects of their language training. ("Ape Studies Help Define Language: An Interview with the Rumbaughs," *Research Resources Reporter*, March 1981, p. 7)

9-50 And the man was exceeding glad. But he asked the Lord God: "Who then *shall* labor in this market place? For am I not management, *being* tall and well formed and pale of hue?" ("The Book of Creation," by Tony Hendra and Sean Kelly, *Playboy*, September 1982, p. 126)

9-51 The headless carcass of a deer, believed to be the buck taken from the Birmingham Zoo over the weekend, has been found off a residential street in Center Point.

Bill Carter, cruelty officer for the Jefferson County Sheriff's office, said zoo officials were to meet with him at the sheriff's office in Fairfield at 9:00 A.M. today to determine if it is Bucky.

"I'm convinced it's the deer that's been missing from the zoo," he said. "The age is right. And its hooves are not worn down, like they would be on an animal that grew up in the wild." ("Dead Deer May Be Zoo's Bucky," *Birmingham News*, November 23, 1983, p. 1)

9-52 Mr. Mayar had told Bridget that the choice of red for the walls [of the pub] was deliberate. It made the people feel hot just looking at it, and so they felt thirsty, and that way they drank more. It was good for business. (*Young Adolf,* by Beryl Bainbridge, p. 29)

9-53 U.S. officials . . . have been pleased by Canada's response to the Soviet downing of a Korean airliner. . . . it has dug up some potent public-relations ammunition: a 1973 quote from Nikolai Podgorny, Soviet president at the time, speaking on the 50th anniversary of Soviet civil aviation. Said Podgorny:"We set human life and well-being above everything else."("Canada: A Warming Trend,"*Newsweek,* September 19, 1983, p. 17)

9-54 How much *can* the brain know? There are perhaps 10^{11} neurons in the brain, the circuit elements and switches that are responsible in their electrical and chemical activity for the functioning of our minds. A typical brain neuron has perhaps a thousand little wires, called dendrites, which connect it with its fellows. If, as seems likely, every bit of information in the brain corresponds to one of these connections, the total number of things knowable by the brain is no more than 10^{14}, one hundred trillion. ("Can We Know the Universe? Reflections on a Grain of Salt," *Broca's Brain: Reflections on the Romance of Science,* by Carl Sagan, p. 15)

9-55 But gas ranges have been standard equipment for decades. Why be concerned now? There are two reasons. In the past, less was known about health effects of air pollutants. But the health hazards of outdoor pollution have been intensively studied over the past 20 years, and scientists now suspect that similar levels of pollutants can be just as hazardous in indoor air. In addition, indoor pollutant levels are apt to be higher now than in the past. Many houses used to be drafty, but as people have tightened up their houses to conserve energy, they have also helped to seal in any contaminants that are created indoors. ("Should You Worry About Gas-Range Emissions?" *Consumer Reports*, January 1984, p. 49)

9-56 The southern part [of Alaska] . . . is bathed by the warm, moist air of the Japanese Current, so it receives up to 220 inches of rain a year and has relatively mild winters. Because of the rain, Southeast Alaska has some of the densest forests, and, around its mountaintops, the biggest iceberg-calving glaciers on the continent. ("At the End of the Earth," by David Rains Wallace, *Wilderness*, Spring 1984, p. 5)

Section 10

Argument Strengths

Introduction

The topic of Section 10 is the strengths of arguments.

In evaluating arguments the logician is interested in how much support the premises give to the conclusion. This evaluation has nothing to do with whether the premises are, in fact, true. It merely concerns the issue: If the premises *were* true, how likely would that make it that the conclusion is true? There are two limiting cases to the amount of support premises can give to a conclusion: (1) The truth of the premises absolutely guarantees that the conclusion is true, in which case the argument is (deductively) valid. (2) The truth of the premises indicates nothing about the truth of the conclusion, in which case the premises are irrelevant to the conclusion. For example:

> *All daffodils are pink, and all pink flowers grow only in Afghanistan; so daffodils grow only in Afghanistan.*

Despite the fact that both the premises and the conclusion of this argument are false, the argument is a valid deductive argument because *if* the premises *were to be true* then the conclusion *would have to be true* also. However, in the "argument"

> *Some hyacinths are blue, therefore oak trees shed their leaves in the fall*

'therefore' indicates that the author of the argument took 'Some hyacinths are blue' to be the reason for claiming that oak trees are deciduous, though this "reason" is totally irrelevant to the "conclusion."

For our present purposes, it is sufficient to recognize three strengths of arguments between these limiting cases: (1) strong—where the premises give good reason for thinking the conclusion to be true, but do not absolutely guarantee it; (2) moderate—where the premises offer a degree of evidence for the conclusion so that it is difficult to know whether to accept the conclusion on those premises alone; and (3) weak—where, although the premises are not irrelevant to the conclusion, they don't provide enough support for us to accept the conclusion on the basis of just those premises.

Each link in the argument can be evaluated for its strength. Because each arrow on an argument diagram represents one link in the argument, the diagrams can be supplemented by writing beside each arrow, in parentheses, an indication of the strength of each link as follows:

D.V.—for deductively valid

Str.—for strong

Mod.—for moderate

Weak—for weak

Nil—where the premises are irrelevant to the conclusion

It is very difficult to pin precise strengths on each of the links in an argument, and probably this fivefold division will be as precise as you will require. However, if you feel the need for a more exact category than the three broad classes of strong, moderate, and weak, you can create intermediate categories such as Mod.-Str.

Once an argument diagram has been constructed for the argument and the strengths indicated on it, it is possible to make an overall assessment of a complex argument. Mostly, this will be obvious from the diagram, but it is important to realize that a serial argument is as strong as its weakest link, whereas a convergent argument is at least as strong as its strongest link. Consider this example:

< ① *The Pacific dogwood flowers in both spring and fall>* and *<* ② *has white flowers>*; (*therefore*) , *<* ③ *some trees have white flowers on them in both the spring and the fall>*. *This is to be expected on other grounds also* —*for example:* < ④ *Daisies have white flowers in both spring and fall>* (*so*) *<* ⑤ *some plants do>*, and *<* ⑥ *trees are just a type of plant>*.

< ② *The Pacific dogwood has a white flower>*

< ⑤ *Some plants have white flowers in both spring and fall>*

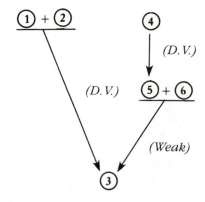

The overall argument is deductively valid because the "left-hand" component of the convergent argument is deductively valid. In the "right-hand" component of the convergent argument, although the link from ④ to ⑤ is deductively valid, because that from ⑤ + ⑥ to ③ is weak, the serial argument from ④ (and ⑥) to ③ is only weak.

Obviously, our main interest in arguments is whether we should accept their conclusions. This decision depends on two assessments: (1) the strength of the argument and (2) the truth of the premises. Clearly, we should not accept a conclusion on the basis of a strong or deductively valid argument if we know that its premises are false. Equally clearly, we should not accept a conclusion on the basis of an argument whose premises are true if the argument has only weak or nil strength. However, the question of the truth of premises is the province of the sciences; in logic we specifically address only the issue of the *strength* of an argument. There is, however, a term that is generally used in logic to denote arguments that both have true premises and are deductively valid—such arguments are called 'sound'.

The author of an argument sometimes includes hints as to how strong she feels her argument is. There are some expressions that indicate a strong argument:

therefore

this proves that;

which demonstrates that;

which shows that.

Other expressions indicate a weak argument:

which suggest that;

this indicates that.

Just as with inference indicator words, such expressions can be helpful but they can also be misleading. We should not take the author's assessment of her argument at face value. Human nature being what it is, we must expect an author to have a favorable view of her argument. So expressions that indicate a strong argument should be taken with a grain of salt, whereas if the author herself is prepared to use an expression that indicates a weak argument, we might expect this to be a realistic assessment.

There is a peculiar problem with one set of expressions that can indicate argument strength—words like 'probably', 'must', and 'possibly'. Often these words can be seen either as assessment words attaching to the inference indicators or as parts of the conclusions. For example, consider the following argument:

> *Plant breeders have succeeded in producing yellow tomatoes, pink grapefruit, and flowers of all sorts of unnatural colors, so* possibly *one day they will breed a day-glow orange snowdrop.*

There are two different ways in which we might construe this argument: (a) with 'so' as the inference indicator and '*Possibly* one day plant breeders will breed a day-glow orange snowdrop' as conclusion or (b) with 'so possibly' as the inference indicator and 'One day plant breeders will breed a day-glow orange snowdrop' as the conclusion. Which interpretation we choose is really immaterial. Interpretation (a) is a strong argument to a weak conclusion; interpretation (b) is a weak argument to a strong conclusion: six of one, half a dozen of the other.

Two texts that have useful discussions of the strengths of arguments are:

Stephen N. Thomas, *Practical Reasoning in Natural Language*, 2nd ed., Ch. 2–1

Robert Baum, *Logic*, 2nd ed., pp. 95–111

Section 10: Instructions

The following arguments contain words that indicate something about argument strength.

Analyze the arguments (making a mental note of the author's assessment of the strength of his argument) and include strength indicators on the argument diagram.

There are relatively few examples in this section because practice with determining argument strengths can be had with any of the examples in Sections 6 through 9. Review the analyses you made of examples in these earlier sections, noting the authors' assessment of argument strength (if any), and add strength indicators to your argument diagrams. Analyze further examples from Sections 6 through 9, including strength indicators on the diagrams.

Section 10: Exercises

10-1 I am fascinated by the point—which I stress in my book *The Dragons of Eden*—that the pain of childbirth is especially marked in human mothers because of the enormous recent growth of the brain in the last few million years. It would seem that our intelligence is the source of our unhappiness in an almost literal way; but it would also imply that our unhappiness is the source of our strength as a species. ("The Amniotic Universe," *Broca's Brain: Reflections on the Romance of Science*, by Carl Sagan, p. 307)

*10-2 "By taking off and landing at night, you've proven that the [space] shuttle [Challenger] is capable of operating under most any condition," President Reagan told the crew. ("Newsmakers," *Newsweek*, September 19, 1983, p. 49)

*10-3 Now, did Adam have a navel? Probably not, simply because the navel is a remnant of the normal birth process, and not of maturity or functionality. Therefore, for God to have created him with one would indeed be deception, because it would convey misleading information. ("Starlight and the Age of the Universe," by Richard Niessen, *Impact*, July 1983, p. iv)

10-4 Secretaries and clerical workers are by and large unable to bargain collectively to secure their rights. As the "office of the future" comes more and more to resemble the factory of the past, however, office workers may organize as factory workers did before them. This could be one result of the computer revolution least welcome to many who have heralded its coming. ("Brave New Office," by Claudia Mills, *QQ-Report from the Center for Philosophy & Public Policy*, Summer 1983, p. 14)

10-5 This list is partial, thus probably unfair. (Comment at the beginning of the "Gear Suppliers" section of the Appendix in *Walking Softly in the Wilderness*, by John Hart, p. 426)

10-6 Salt cod can be transported by ship without becoming mouldy or spoiling otherwise; on land it will last for several years. Smoked and pickled herring keep well too, but these processes are a trifle more complicated than drying or even salting and may therefore be presumed to have been developed later. ("Cod," *Food: An Authoritative and Visual History and Dictionary of the Foods of the World*, by Waverley Root, p. 85)

10-7 Some people think couponers and refunders are very tight with a dollar and once they save a few cents, they never let go. This convention was proof that this isn't so. It was held at the Miracle Mile Resort complex's luxurious Gulfside Inn, right on the beach. More than 170 refunders came from all over the Gulf Coast, and most of them had ocean-front rooms! ("Coupon Convention Traders Positive, Progressive, Pleased," by Martin Sloane, *Birmingham News*, November 2, 1983, p. 4D)

10-8 Do woodpeckers suffer from headaches?

Probably not, according to the people who worry about the problem. If they did, the birds would presumably stop slamming their beaks into trees hundreds of times a day. ("Why Woodpeckers Don't Need Helmets," *Science 80*, September/October 1980, p. 93)

*10-9 Sartre has been called the conscience of his generation. Unquestionably he was too often wrong for that. ("Inadvertent Guru to an Age," *Time*, April 28, 1980, p. 39)

10-10 Similar "meaningful coincidences" can be said to occur when there is a vital necessity for an individual to know about, say, a relative's death, or some lost possession. In a great many cases such information has been revealed by means of extrasensory perception. This seems to suggest that abnormal random phenomena may occur when a vital need or urge is aroused; and this in turn might explain why a species of animals, under great pressure or in great need, could produce "meaningful" (but *acausal*) changes in its outer material structure. ("Science and the Unconscious," by M. L. Franz, in *Man and His Symbols*, by Carl G. Jung et al., p. 380)

*10-11 Gastronomic writers repeat endlessly that Cicero was so called because he had a wart on his nose the size of a chick-pea (*cicer*, in Latin); but this can hardly be so . . . for Cicero was not his nickname, it was his family name, which antedated his wart by countless generations. ("Chick-pea," *Food: An Authoritative and Visual History and Dictionary of the Foods of the World*, by Waverley Root, p. 69)

10-12 These trends demonstrate that the housing market can respond, albeit slowly, to environmental constraints and demographic and social changes. The nature of these changes suggests a future for housing quite unlike the immediate past. ("Smaller Houses for Smaller Households," by Bruce Stokes, *Sierra*, September/October, 1982, p. 47)

10-13 Light, travelling at 186,000 miles per second, will travel about 6 trillion miles in one year. This distance is called one light-year. There are galaxies that are alleged to be billions of light-years distance from us in space. This means that the light, which left the galaxies 5 billion years ago, should just now be reaching us. This would seem to indicate that the universe and the creation must be at least 5 billion years old or else we wouldn't be seeing this light. ("Starlight and the Age of the Universe," by Richard Niessen, *Impact*, July 1983, p. i)

10-14 "That's what I mean," he said; "I sore that pitcha. 'Doctor Jack-o'-lantern and Mr. Hide.'"

There was a burst of wild, delighted laughter and a chorus of correction: "Doctor *Jekyll!*"

He was unable to speak over the noise. Miss Price was on her feet, furious. "It's a *perfectly natural mistake!*" she was saying. "There's no reason for any of you to be so rude. Go on, Vincent, and please excuse this very silly interruption." The laughter subsided, but the class continued to shake their heads derisively from side to side. It hadn't, of course, been a perfectly natural mistake at all; for one thing it proved that he was a hopeless dope, and for another it proved that he was lying. ("Doctor Jack-o'-lantern," *Eleven Kinds of Loneliness*, by Richard Yates, p. 12)

10-15 A microbiologist at the University of California, Davis, has detected similarities between fluids in human blood and fluids found in nodules attached to soybeans. Further studies may show that humans are distantly related to soybeans. ("Our Cousin the Soybean," *Theorist*, Fall 1983, p. 4)

10-16   The plot to "transfer" a $1.5 million VAX 11/782 high-speed computer and special pro-
duction machinery suggests that Moscow still needs U.S. help to design and manufac-
ture superchips that will be the heart of the weapons of the 1990s. But the scam's partial
success also underscored the inadequacy of Washington's export-licensing procedures.
("Moscow's Computer Capers," by David M. Alperon, *Newsweek*, January 2, 1984, p.
19)

10-17   Several samples of the Cooper 270 came with the indoor and outdoor scales reversed.
That assembly defect didn't impede installation, and it wouldn't fool anyone for long.
But it was an annoyance, signifying sloppy workmanship. ("Indoor/Outdoor Ther-
mometers," *Consumer Reports*, February 1984, p. 80)

10-18   "One day I went out to gather wood for the fire and when I returned I found that Mr.
Swan, the oldest man in the party, had been struck on the head and killed, and the
remainder of the party were in the act of cutting up the body preparatory to eating
it. . . .

"This food only lasted a few days, and I suggested that Miller be the next victim
because of the large amount of flesh he carried." (Packer, quoted in "Alfred G. Packer,
the 'Maneater', Who Murdered His Five Companions in the Mountains of Colorado,
Ate Their Bodies and Stole Their Money," in Duke's *Celebrated Criminal Cases of
America*, quoted in *The Thin Man*, by Dashiell Hammett, pp. 70-71)

10-19 Superior taste, superb quality and sophisticated flavors plus the deliciously rich creamy texture only the world's best ice cream could possibly have! (Ad for Haagen-Dazs ice cream, *Essence*, May 1983, p. 100)

10-20 I like to whistle songs, so if the moon were to disappear, some of the songs I like would disappear. Songs like "Harvest Moon" . . . "By the Light of the Silvery Moon." (Mitch Heider, "All Things Considered," NPR, WBHM, March 2, 1984)

10-21 Jackie Cooper survived the battered child part in the original *Champ* to become a successful TV actor and producer, so presumably Ricky Schroeder [who plays the battered child part in the remake of *Champ*] will not be permanently scarred. ("Films," by Robert Hatch, *Nation*, April 28, 1979, p. 275)

10-22 John Cabot sailed from Bristol to Newfoundland in 1497, and an entry in the Crown's Privy Purse expenses proves it: "To hym who found the New Isle 10 pounds." ("A Short History," *Canada Today/d'aujourd'hui*, 1984, No. 1, p. 5)

Section 11

Valid Deductive Arguments: Propositional Logic

Introduction

Having covered general techniques for analyzing arguments, the remaining sections concern special types of arguments. In Sections 11 and 12, the topic is deductively valid arguments. The examples of this section are concerned with propositional (or sentential) logic.

The study of deductively valid arguments is a large and specialized field. In its most complete form it requires learning special formal languages. Even within this special field there are recognized and generally agreed-upon techniques for demonstrating the validity of only some of the arguments known to be valid. There are, however, two types of arguments that can be dealt with successfully—and it is those that we consider here. One of these types of argument is the subject matter of propositional logic.

An essential in propositional logic is the ability to recognize the simple sentences within compound sentences. For this reason, you should review the material covered in Section 5 at this point.

Propositional logic tells us there are various argument forms that are known to be valid (and others that are known to be invalid). One valid argument form, called 'modus ponens,' is as follows:

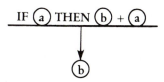

This argument diagram shows that modus ponens is a linked argument form with two premises, one of them a conditional. It is a diagram of an argument *form* because rather than containing the numbers of particular sentences, it contains variables— (a) , (b) —just like the variables of algebra. To obtain a particular argument from the argument form, particular sentences are substituted for the variables, the same sentence being substituted for the same variable wherever it occurs. This allows us to define the modus ponens argument form as follows: A modus ponens argument is a linked argument, one of whose premises is a conditional, the other being the sentence that is the antecedent of that conditional, and the conclusion being the sentence that is the consequent of the conditional. Because the argument form modus ponens is valid, any argument that has this structure is a deductively valid argument. For example:

> *If San Diego is in Alaska then it snows in the winter in San Diego; so it snows there in the winter, because it is in Alaska*

is a valid argument (even though one of its premises and its conclusion are, of course, false). 'It snows there [in San Diego] in the winter' is the conclusion; and the premises are 'If San Diego is in Alaska then it snows in the winter in San Diego' and 'It [San Diego] is in Alaska'. One of these premises is a conditional, the other is the antecedent of the conditional, and the conclusion is the consequent of the conditional. Thus the San Diego argument is a valid deductive argument of the form modus ponens.

Following are some valid argument forms in propositional logic and passages that give straightforward examples of these forms, where the premises are all given first and separated by commas, followed by '; thus ', followed by the conclusion.

Six Valid Propositional Argument Forms

Modus Ponens

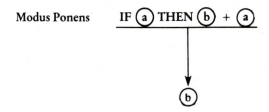

For example:

> *If Seattle is west of Denver then it's west of Cincinnati, Seattle is west of Denver; thus Seattle is west of Cincinnati.*

Modus Tollens

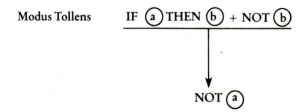

For example:

> *If Chicago is at the bottom of Lake Michigan then Chicago taxis would have to be submarines, Chicago taxis are not submarines; thus Chicago is not at the bottom of Lake Michigan.*

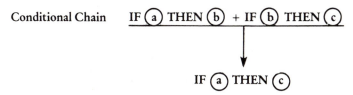

For example:

> *If Vancouver has more rain than Biloxi then Biloxi has more sun than Vancouver, if Biloxi has more sun than Vancouver then Biloxi's summers must be hotter than Vancouver's; thus if Vancouver has more rain than Biloxi then Biloxi's summers must be hotter than Vancouver's.*

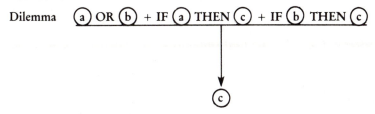

For example:

> *Pass Christian is in Mississippi or Louisiana, if it is in Mississippi then it is in Dixie, if it is in Louisiana then it is in Dixie; thus Pass Christian is in Dixie.*

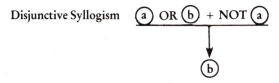

For example:

> *Reno is in New Hampshire or Nevada, it is not in New Hampshire; thus Reno is in Nevada.*

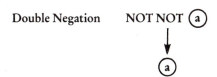

For example:

> *It is not true that New Orleans is not a Gulf port; thus New Orleans is a*
> *Gulf port.*

Because of some important similarities and differences between them, it is important to distinguish among modus ponens, modus tollens, and the following argument forms.

Two Invalid Propositional
Argument Forms

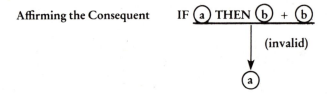

Affirming the Consequent   IF (a) THEN (b) + (b)

(invalid)

(a)

For example:

> *If Lincoln is in South Dakota then it is on the prairies, Lincoln is on the*
> *prairies; thus it is in South Dakota.*

Denying the Antecedent   IF (a) THEN (b) + NOT (a)

(invalid)

NOT (b)

For example:

> *If Plains is a great U.S. city then it must be south of the Canadian*
> *border. Plains is not a great U.S. city; thus it is not south of the*
> *Canadian border.*

These are only some of the valid and invalid propositional argument forms, but they are some of the ones most commonly encountered in everyday arguments. As with any argument, the premises and conclusion of propositional arguments can occur in any order in a passage, with or without indicator expressions. Similarly, complex propositional arguments can be built from these component building blocks. Also, propositional arguments can have missing premises and/or conclusions. Indeed, missing conclusions are not at all uncommon in fairly simple deductive arguments because given the premises in such an argument, it is usually so obvious what the conclusion is that the author of the argument may not trouble to state it.

There are many texts having very complete treatments of symbolic propositional logic that advance the discussion far beyond what is given here. Note that the argument forms just described may be given different names in other texts. Two texts that discuss propositional argument forms at a level similar to the preceding discussion are as follows:

Stephen N. Thomas, *Practical Reasoning in Natural Language*, 2nd ed., Ch. 2–3

Monroe C. Beardsley, *Writing with Reason*, Ch. 10

Section 11: Instructions

Analyze the propositional arguments in the examples, as follows:

1. Mark up the passage by (a) circling inference indicators, (b) underlining words used to form compound sentences from simple sentences, and (c) angle bracketing and numbering simple sentences (where angle bracketing on the passage is not adequate to clearly specify a simple sentence, write out the sentence below the passage, numbering it and enclosing it in angle brackets).

2. Draw an argument diagram. Any premise or conclusion that is a compound sentence should be expressed in the standard form by giving the numbers for the component simple sentences and writing, in upper-case letters, the logical words used to form the compound sentences.

3. If the argument is a simple example of one of the propositional argument forms detailed earlier, write the name of the argument form beside the argument diagram.

4. Beside the arrows representing the argument links indicate whether the argument is valid or invalid by writing, in parentheses, 'D.V.' or 'Inval.' respectively.

Here is one example:

It's a shame, but it is easy to see what the fate of the Indiana dunes will be: if < ① they are used for construction sand > < ② they will be gone within forty years >, < ② as they will also > if < ③ they are left to be blown into Lake Michigan by the prevailing winds >, and < ① they will either be used for construction sand > or < ③ blown into Lake Michigan >.

< ① The Indiana dunes are used for construction sand >

< ② The Indiana dunes will be gone within forty years >

< ③ The Indiana dunes are left to blow into Lake Michigan by the prevailing winds >

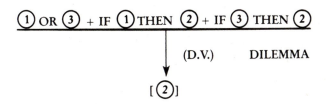

Another example is as follows:

If < ① Tampa is in California> then < ② it is in a state that grows a lot of oranges>, so <not ② it is not in a state that grows a lot of oranges>, because <not ① it is not in California>.

< ② Tampa is in a state that grows a lot of oranges>

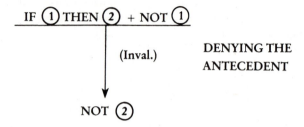

IF ① THEN ② + NOT ①

(Inval.)

DENYING THE ANTECEDENT

NOT ②

Section 11: Exercises

11–1 The Moral Majority's Rev. Jerry Falwell relies more peculiarly on Christian authority. He claims that Jesus Christ favored the death penalty. On the Cross, Falwell says, he could have spoken up: "If ever there was a platform for our Lord to condemn capital punishment, that was it. He did not." ("An Eye for an Eye," by Kurt Andersen, *Time*, January 24, 1983, p. 36)

11–2 If food did not exist it would be well-nigh impossible to get certain types off the phone, as one would be unable to say, "Look, I've got to run but let's have dinner sometime soon." ("Food for Thought and Vice Versa," *Metropolitan Life*, by Fran Lebowitz, pp. 110–111)

*11–3 Either this is the best space game ever, or my living room is going 156 m.p.h. (Ad for Intellivision Star Strike, *Playboy*, August 1982, p. 173)

11-4   If the Winter Olympics are a wholesome spectator sport, then frostbite is an aphrodisi-ac. (Donald Caul, commenting on the Winter Olympics 1984, "All Things Considered," NPR, WBHM, February 12, 1984)

11-5   Nobody doesn't like Sara Lee. (Ad for Sara Lee frozen bakery products, WBRC-Television, Birmingham, Alabama, February 27, 1982)

11-6   VITAMINS FOR SUPERIOR HEALTH

If the RDA's were adequate, then increased intake would not result in increased health benefits. Yet Dr. Emanuel Cheraskin and his University of Alabama colleague, Dr. W. M. Ringsdorf, have found higher intake does result in better health.

Dr. Cheraskin's group studied the number of clinical symptoms of a group of people versus their nutrient intake, and determined with every nutrient tested so far, that levels appreciably higher than the RDA resulted in the fewest symptoms, therefore, producing the best health. (*The Best of Forum*, 1980, p. 3)

*11-7 Q: Zsa Zsa Gabor, who recently got married for the eighth time, gave her age as 54. If that's true, she was only 5 when she entered and won the Miss Hungary beauty title in 1933. How old is Zsa Zsa really?—Norma Singer, Playa del Rey, Calif.

A: Best guess: 66 or 67. Incidentally, her eighth marriage lasted three days.

(Walter Scott's Personality Parade, *Parade*, May 30, 1982, p. 2)

11-8 When your body loses heat, you get cold. If you're cold, you're uncomfortable. And if you're uncomfortable, you won't sleep. (*Backpacking*, by Michael Sandi, p. 185)

11-9 Q: In his book "Witness to Power," John Ehrlichman accuses Dan Rather of being lazy, careless in checking his facts, and calls him a reporter who lacks objectivity. How much truth is there in Ehrlichman's charge, or is it just a case of sour grapes?—Nicholas P. Criscuolo, New Haven, Conn.

A: Rather may have weaknesses, but laziness, carelessness and lack of objectivity aren't among them.

(Walter Scott's Personality Parade, *Parade*, July 18, 1982, p. 2)

11-10 "If our whole production were trash, would the whole world ask for more and more of it . . .?" (From Anbot de Villaine [coproprietor of Le Domaine de la Romance—Conti] in a private letter to Robert Finigan, reprinted in *Robert Finigan's Private Guide to Wines*, April 26, 1979, California edition, p. 41)

11-11 In fact, I'd say that 100 years from now the river will probably be clean as a whistle, drinkable. But it can happen one of two ways: Either the human race will get together, straighten up and fly right—eliminating war, poverty, racism, sexism, alienation, and pollution—or it will not get rid of these things. In which case we'll be back to the Stone Age, and there won't be enough people alive to pollute it. ("Song of the Clearwater," by Pete Seeger, *Parade*, November 26, 1978, p. 7)

11-12 When oil companies make money, they drill for oil. When they drill, they need steel. When they need steel, they need steelworkers. Hey, when oil companies make money, they make jobs. (Ad for Shell Oil, *Birmingham News*, November 26, 1979, p. 6C)

11-13 Three human fetuses were discovered inside a garbage truck yesterday. An employee of BFI (Browning-Ferris Industries) Waste Systems found the fetuses about 9 A.M. while scrubbing the container of a truck at the company's garage at 31 First Avenue North.

All the fetuses were less than 20 weeks into gestation "and therefore under the laws of Alabama would be considered tissue specimens rather than stillborn," Deputy Coroner Jay Glass said.

Autopsies showed all the fetuses had come from spontaneous or induced abortions performed either at hospitals or other medically approved institutions.

The institution or agency that disposed of the fetuses is not known, Glass said.

Homicide investigators were called; it later was discovered no laws had been violated. "We will not be investigating it all," said Lt. John Davis, head of Birmingham's Homicide unit. "Under state law, unless there's a birth, they can't be killed in a homicide." ("Human Fetuses Found in Garbage Truck," *Birmingham Post-Herald*, August 4, 1982, p. E1. Reprinted by permission)

11-14 Try not to nail in a staight line along a board, but rather in some kind of pattern. This is to avoid having too many nails enter the same line of grain, which might cause the wood to split. (*Illustrated Basic Carpentry*, by Graham Blackburn, p. 91)

11-15 Piglet said that Tigger *was* very Bouncy, and that if they could think of a way of unbouncing him it would be a Very Good Idea.

"Well, I've got an idea," said Rabbit, "and here it is. We take Tigger for a long explore, somewhere where he's never been before, and we loose him there, and next morning we find him again, and—mark my words—he'll be a different Tigger altogether."

"Why?" said Pooh.

"Because, he'll be a Humble Tigger. Because he'll be a Sad Tigger, a Melancholy Tigger, a Small and Sorry Tigger, an Oh-Rabbit-I-am-glad-to-see-you Tigger. That's why." (*The House at Pooh Corner*, by A. A. Milne, pp. 106–109)

*11-16 You are either good or bad, and both are dangerous. Go away. (*The Looking Glass War,* by John Le Carre, p. 269)

11-17 Were the U.S. genuinely in pursuit of justice, a destabilization campaign against South Africa or the El Salvadorean Government (as opposed to its enemies) would have toppled the incumbent regimes long ago. (Letter from Philip Hall, *Manchester Guardian Weekly,* November 13, 1983, p. 2)

11-18 What is literature. (For some fellow Sinologists, bent on doing a *scientific* study of literature and ever wary of committing the sin of *subjective* value judgments, the sole fact that "it" has appeared in print seems a sufficient criterion: I always wonder why they do not include the telephone directory in their sphere of scholarly inquiry.) ("Introduction, by Simon Leys," in *The Execution of Mayor Yin and Other Stories from the Great Proleterian Cultural Revolution,* by Jo-Hsi Chen, p. xvi)

11-19 Some people dream of relaxing on a secluded island.

Others dream of more lavish surroundings.

In the Bahamas you can have either.

(Ad for the Bahamas, *Better Homes and Gardens*, August 1979, p. 61)

11-20 If you can find the trash can, you can run a computer. (Ad for Apple computers, *Business Week*, October 17, 1983, p. 48)

11-21 If democratically elected civilian leaders *fail to deliver*, protests and turbulence seem sure to follow. If that happens, don't be surprised if there is replay of a familiar Latin American drama—*a military coup*. ("No Quick Cure for Argentina," *U.S. News & World Report*, October 31, 1983, p. 34)

11-22 If we made them look like other loudspeakers . . . that's all they would sound like. (Ad for Design Acoustics, showing some unusual-looking speakers, *Audio*, November 1983, p. 100)

11-23 At this point an annoying, though obvious question intrudes. If Skinner's thesis is false, then there is no point in his having written the book or in our reading it. But, if his thesis is true, then there is also no point in his having written the book or our reading it. ("The Case Against B. F. Skinner," by Noam Chomsky, *New York Review of Books*, December 30, 1971, p. 20)

11-24 If oxygen were in the primitive atmosphere, life could not have arisen because the chemical precursors would have been destroyed through oxidation; if oxygen were not in the primitive atmosphere, then neither would have been ozone, and if ozone were not present to shield the chemical precursors of life from ultraviolet light, life could not have arisen. (*The Creation-Evolution Controversy*, by R. L. Wyson, p. 212)

*11-25 Winnie-The-Pooh from a defensive reaction mechanism stems, employing the projective technique of inversion of affect: the feared bear becomes the loved bear, the enemy becomes the inseparable-friend. Thus, in daydream the severely phobic A. A. Milne makes a pathetic, clinically most interesting attempt, discovered by me, to deny his phobia and rid himself of his obsessive traits. This diagnosis, as well as explaining the anxiety reduction function of many chapters in the Milne book, offers a general clue to further psycholiterary mysteries, as will be seen. (" 'A. A. Milne's Honey-Balloon-Pit-Gun-Tail-Bathtub Complex' by Karl Anschsuung, M.D.," *The Pooh Perplex*, by Frederick C. Crews, pp. 128–129)

11-26   When you make it better, you can guarantee it is better.

      The proof of our superior writing ability is our superior guarantee. If your Paper Mate pen ever fails to perform to your satisfaction, send it back and we'll give you a replacement. (Ad for Paper Mate Pens, *Reader's Digest*, December 1982, p. 15)

11-27   If he [Marvin] had had teeth he would have gritted them at this point. He hadn't. He didn't. (*Life, the Universe and Everything*, by Douglas Adams, p. 53)

11-28   You, as author, are answerable for all permissions–for obvious reasons. No publisher could undertake the immense task for all his authors, and if he cannot do it for all, he cannot do it for any. (*Wadsworth Author's Guide*, p. 52)

11-29   "Where there is water there are fishes," wrote Dr. Gareth Nelson of the Department of Ichthyology at the American Museum of Natural History, "and where there are fishes they can be caught." ("Fish," *Food: An Authoritative and Visual History and Dictionary of the Foods of the World*, by Waverley Root, p. 132)

11-30   FAVORS HORSE RACING

We need more revenue. Horse racing and the state lottery bill will give us the revenue. . . .

Bob White,
648 Alabama Avenue.
("Reader's Opinions," *Birmingham News*, February 8, 1984, p. 8A)

11-31   If one must have an animal in a place like Manhattan, and it seems that one must, a camel seemed the least troublesome choice. So I bought a camel. ("Beastly Manhattan," *The Rescue of Miss Yaskell and Other Pipe Dreams*, by Russell Baker, p. 33)

11-32 Maxwell calculated the speed at which such a wave [an electromagnetic wave] would travel and found it agreed exactly with the speed of light. The coincidence was too striking to be ignored. Maxwell concluded that light itself must be an electromagnetic wave. (*Physics for Poets*, by Robert H. March, p. 112)

11-33 "If it was a coincidence, then my name," roared the voice, "is not Agrajag!!!"

"And presumably," said Arthur, "you would claim that that *was* your name."

"Yes!" hissed Agrajag, as if he had just completed a rather deft syllogism. (*Life, the Universe, and Everything*, by Douglas Adams, p. 121)

11-34 If "Providence" is garbage, and it is, it's high-class garbage. ("The Last Romantic," a review by Peter S. Prescott of *Providence*, by Anita Brookner, *Newsweek*, February 27, 1984, p. 71)

11-35 From a "For Better or for Worse" cartoon strip:

Frame 1—Mike:

"Be nice to Brad Luggsworth! What does Mom think I am—crazy?!!"

Frame 2—Mike:

"If I asked him to be friends or somethin'—he'd MASH me!!"

Frame 3—Friend 1:
"It's worth a try, Mike!"
        Friend 2: "What have you got to lose?"

Frame 4—Friend 1:
"Yeah!—He's just gonna mash you anyways!"

(*Birmingham News*, November 24, 1983, p. 9H)

11-36   Your finger knows how to point, doesn't it? Good. Then you can master Apple's newest
        32-bit wonder, Macintosh. (Ad for Apple computers, *Nutshell*, Spring 1984, p. 5)

Section 12

Valid Deductive Arguments: Quantificational Logic

Introduction

The examples of this section are arguments in the domain of quantificational (or predicate) logic—the other main established and noncontroversial area of deductive logic. In propositional logic, the validity of arguments hinges on relations between complete sentences. In quantificational logic, the validity of arguments depends upon factors internal to a sentence. Thus we begin the discussion of quantificational logic by examining some of the internal structures of sentences.

First, it is necessary to distinguish between two types of subject-predicate sentences: those where the subject is the name of an individual (or the names of individuals) and those where the subject is a quantified expression. Examples of subject-predicate sentences where the subject (shown here in italics) is a named individual are the following:

Milton Friedman is an economist.

The Dow Jones Index is a stock market index.

I.T.&T. and G.E. are two healthy stocks.

Apple is a rapidly growing company.

These examples make it clear that names of individuals are not necessarily names of people. Examples of sentences with quantified subject expressions (again italicized) are the following:

Any stock that goes up has to come down.

All money market funds are risky investments.

Some banks are run by questionable directors.

No savings and loan association has branches in every state.

The subject expressions in these sentences contain the *quantity* terms 'any', 'all', 'some', and 'no'.

Second, it is important to recognize that predicates and subjects that are quantified expressions implicitly refer to various classes of things. Some of the classes referred to in the predicates of the preceding sentences are the class of economists, the class of companies that are rapidly growing, the class of things that have to come down, and the class of things run by questionable directors. The classes referred to in the quantified subject expressions in the preceding sentences are the class of stocks that go up, the class of money market funds, the class of banks, and the class of savings and loan associations.

The quantity terms in quantified subject expressions say something about how much of the subject class the predicate holds true of. For example, 'has to come down' hold true of *every*thing in the class of stocks that go up; 'are run by questionable directors' is true of *some* things in the class of banks; and 'have branches in every state' is true of *no*thing in the class of savings and loan associations.

We can draw diagrams—called 'Venn diagrams'—to represent any of these types of sentences. There are two essential elements to a Venn diagram: the key and the diagram proper. In the key we enter a single upper-case letter abbreviation for any class term that occurs in the sentence or sentences to be diagramed and a single lower-case letter abbreviation for every name of an individual. The Venn diagram proper consists of a rectangle, and within the rectangle as many overlapping circles as there are class terms in the key, each circle labeled with one of the class abbreviations. For example, for diagraming the sentence 'All money market funds are risky investments', the setup is as follows:

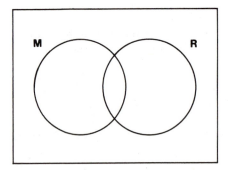

KEY
M abbreviates the class of money market funds
R abbreviates the class of risky investments

To diagram the content of a sentence on a Venn diagram, it is necessary to understand that everything in the universe is represented by a point in the rectangle: Everything that is a money market fund is represented by a point within the circle M; everything that is not a money market fund is represented by a point outside the circle M; and so on.

Now to say that all money market funds are risky investments is to say that everything in the class M is also in the class R. Thus the part of circle M outside circle R is empty—that is, there is no money market fund that is not a risky investment. This is diagramed by shading the area of circle M that does not overlap with circle R—the shading indicating that the shaded area of the diagram is empty:

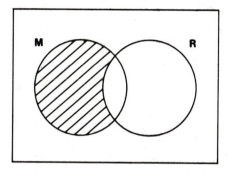

KEY
M abbreviates the class of money market funds
R abbreviates the class of risky investments

Similarly, 'No savings and loan association has branches in every state' can be diagramed as follows:

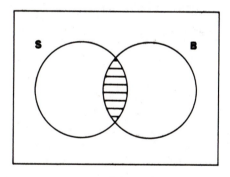

KEY
S abbreviates the class of savings and loan associations
B abbreviates the class of things that have branches in every state

The sentence says that anything in class S is not in class B; thus the overlap of circles S and B is empty.

The quantity terms 'all' and 'none' represent the two extremes; 'some' represents an intermediate position. Logicians treat 'some' as if it were equivalent to 'at least one'. Moreover, although there are other "intermediate" quantity terms (such as 'a few', 'most', 'several', and 'many') that have slightly different meanings, logicians disregard the small differences between them and treat them all as if they were equivalent to 'some'. Sentences having these quantity expressions are diagramed using '*', which indicates that there is some element in the area in the diagram in which the asterisk occurs. Thus 'Some banks are run by questionable directors' is diagramed as follows:

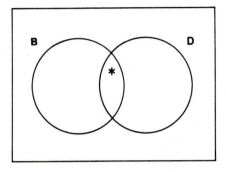

KEY
B abbreviates the class of banks
D abbreviates the class of things run by questionable directors

Although there are English variants on some of the quantity terms (for example, 'any' and 'every'), all sentences with quantified subject expressions can be diagramed in one of these ways: using the techniques of overlapping circles for each class term, shading to indicate absence of elements, and asterisking to indicate presence of at least one element.

Sentences that have names in the subject position can also be dealt with easily. Such sentences say that there is a member of a certain class (which can be indicated by asterisking) and they give the name of the thing (which is indicated by writing the abbreviation for the name beside the asterisk). For example, 'Milton Friedman is an economist' is diagramed.

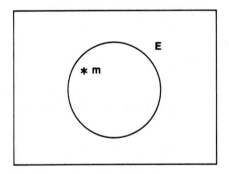

KEY
m abbreviates Milton Friedman
E abbreviates the class of economist

Multiple subjects and predicates can, of course, easily be handled by simple extension of these techniques. 'I.T.&T. and G.E. are two healthy stocks' would appear as follows:

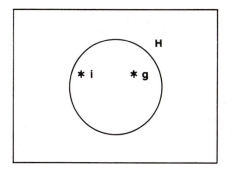

KEY
i abbreviates I.T.&T.
g abbreviates G.E.
H abbreviates the class of healthy
stocks

And a diagram of 'Some mortgage companies operate in South America and in the Far East' would be

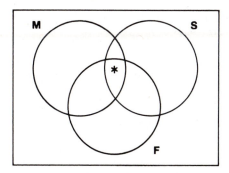

KEY
M abbreviates the class of mortgage companies
S abbreviates the class of things that operate in South America
F abbreviates the class of things that operate in the Far East

Venn diagrams allow an easy test of validity of a quantificational argument. All of the premises of an argument are diagramed on the same diagram. If we would have to make any additions to the diagram to enter on it the content of the conclusion, then the argument is not valid. If no additions are necessary for the diagram to express the content of the conclusion, the argument is valid.

For example, the premises of the argument

All stockbrokers are wealthy, and all wealthy people own stock; so all stockbrokers own stock

are diagrammed

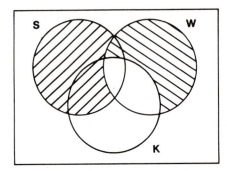

KEY
S abbreviates the class of stockbrokers
W abbreviates the class of wealthy people
K abbreviates the class of things that own stock

and, as nothing would have to be added to the diagram for it to express the content of the conclusion, the argument is valid. However, the premises of the argument

All economists are traitors, and all traitors are enemies of the state; thus all enemies of the state are economists

are diagrammed

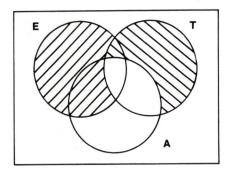

KEY
E abbreviates the class of economists
T abbreviates the class of traitors
A abbreviates the class of enemies of the state

and as further shading is required for the diagram to contain the content 'all enemies of the state are economists', the argument is not deductively valid.

Because the treatment here of Venn diagraming is necessarily brief, we have had to avoid or gloss over some difficulties and controversies. For a complete grasp of these techniques, a more comprehensive text must be consulted. Good treatments are given in the following:

Evelyn M. Barker, *Everyday Reasoning*, Ch. 6

Robert J. Fogelin, *Understanding Arguments*, Ch. 7

Finally, it should be noted that, although the techniques employed in symbolic propositional logic are continuous with those discussed in Section 11, techniques very different from Venn diagraming are used in symbolic logic to prove validity of quantificational arguments.

Section 12: Instructions

Most of the passages that follow contain quantificational arguments. Such exercises are to be tested for validity. A few of the passages are just a series of quantificational statements. These exercises can be used as practice in Venn diagraming.

Test for validity of quantificational argument by doing the following:

1. Mark up the passage by (a) circling inference indicators and (b) angle bracketing significant sentences.
2. Write beneath the passage the significant sentences that are either unstated or inadequately specified by angle bracketing on the passage.
3. Draw a Venn diagram for the premises of the argument.
4. Check to see whether any addition would have to be made for the diagram to express the content of the conclusion: If additions are required, the argument is invalid; if not, it is valid.

For example:

All savings and loan institutions offer Super Now accounts, and every institution that offers Super Now accounts also has IRAs; so all savings and loan institutions have IRAs.

This should be marked up as follows:

<All savings and loan institutions offer Super Now accounts>, and <every institution that offers Super Now accounts also has IRAs>; (so) <all savings and loan institutions have IRAs>.

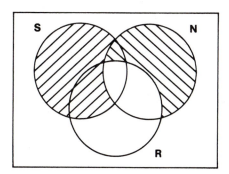

KEY
S abbreviates the class of savings and loan institutions
N abbreviates the class of institutions that offer Super Now accounts
R abbreviates the class of institutions that have IRAs

Once the content of the premises has been diagramed on the Venn diagram, nothing further is required to diagram the content of the conclusion. Therefore, the argument is valid.

Section 12: Exercises

12-1 "We are not flying into that and there's no way round it," he [Senator John Glenn] told the small band of aides and correspondents travelling with his party. There was no argument from the flight crew or the campaign party. When one of the world's greatest pilots says it isn't safe, you don't fly. ("Glenn's 'Right Stuff' Versus Mondale's Machine," by Alex Brummer, *Manchester Guardian Weekly*, October 23, 1983, p. 7)

*12-2 Add naught to MacNaughton—because you don't dilute a great Canadian Whisky. (Billboard ad, I-20 southbound, Birmingham, Alabama, October 1983)

12-3 The magazine you are reading is protected by the First Amendment.

Radio and television are *not*!

The First Amendment guarantees the rights of free speech and freedom of the press.

(Ad by the Mutual Broadcasting System, *Newsweek*, September 19, 1983, p. 80)

12-4 Grandmother disapproved of candy . . . because children liked it and children should perforce not have anything they like. ("R Is for Romantic," *An Alphabet for Gourmets*, in *The Art of Eating*, by M. F. K. Fisher, p. 679)

12-5 PERKINS SHOWS CLASS

Ray Perkins has carried on another Alabama coaching tradition—not saying the officials cost the Tide a game . . . And that shows class. ("NewsBreak," *Birmingham News*, October 12, 1983, p. 1)

*12-6 Madelyn, a Cherokee Indian, came to ICO 12 years ago when the Boy Scouts of America told her she could not be a leader of her son's scouting troup because, as a woman, she would not be able to lead a 12-mile hike! ("Beyond City Limits: An Outings Program for Urban Kids," by Susan A. Suchman, *Sierra*, September/October 1983, p. 72)

12-7 It should be noted that atonia and paralysis are not identical. Paralysis can be the result of several conditions other than atonia. If the muscles are atonic, however, the animal will necessarily be paralyzed. ("A Window on the Sleeping Brain," by Adrian R. Morrison, *Scientific American*, April 1983, p. 96)

12-8 Risi e bisi is often listed on menus among the soups, and some gastronomic writers dare to call it one. Nonsense! It is served with a fork. Who ever heard of eating soup with a fork? ("Risi e bisi," *The Best of Italian Cooking*, by Waverley Root, p. 219)

12-9 The Occupational Safety and Health Act of 1970 takes as its stated purpose "to assure so far as possible every working man and woman in the nation safe and healthful working conditions." The right to a safe and healthful workplace is already guaranteed by law . . . so office workers whose health is jeopardized by the stampede to computerization should face no new legal and moral battles. ("Brave New Office," by Claudia Mills, *QQ-Report from the Center for Philosophy & Public Policy*, Summer 1983, p. 12)

12-10 Almost 18 months after that confession, the Court of Appeals, Maryland's highest court, ruled in another case that a defendant had to be taken before a court commissioner within 24 hours of arrest, or the state could not use any subsequent confession. McClain was not taken before a commissioner until he had given his confession—24 hours and 12 minutes after the arrest.

The Court of Appeals decided to make its ruling retroactive.

So James McClain is a free man. (Column by Michael Olesker, Baltimore *Sun*, in "Crime and Nonpunishment, U.S.A.," *Reader's Digest*, November 1981, p. 134)

12-11 The . . . chick-pea is not a pea, though it does belong to the same family, the Leguminosae . . . It is also a member of the same subfamily as the pea, the Papilionoideae. ("Chick-pea," *Food: An Authoritative and Visual History and Dictionary of the Foods of the World*, by Waverley Root, p. 69)

12-12 The warranty covers only major structural defects.

HOW defines a "major structural defect" as actual damage to a load-bearing component of the house. . . . in a house with a trussed-roof system, all the load is carried by the outside walls, so no inside wall would be considered load-bearing; no cracks in such a wall would be covered. ("Housing Yourself in the 80's: How Good Are Home Warranties?" *Consumer Reports*, July 1981, p. 407)

12-13   "By taking off and landing at night, you've proven that the [space] shuttle [Challenger] is capable of operating under most any conditions," President Reagan told the crew. ("Newsmakers," *Newsweek*, September 19, 1983, p. 49)

12-14   Now, did Adam have a navel? Probably not, simply because a navel is a remnant of the normal birth process. ("Starlight and the Age of the Universe," by Richard Niessen, *Impact*, July 1983, p. iv)

12-15   Bacardi dark.

It tastes good mixed because

It tastes good unmixed.

(Ad for Bacardi rum, *Newsweek*, March 16, 1981, p. 9)

12-16   The pop operations cannot be applied to the empty stack because such a stack has no elements to delete. (*Data Structures Using Pascal*, by Aaron M. Tenenbaum and Moshe J. Augenstein, p. 60)

*12-17 He [Sartre] did not write like a philosopher either, for he commanded a graceful prose style. ("Inadvertent Guru to an Age," *Time*, April 28, 1980, p. 39)

12-18 Phoenix, Ariz.—The Roman Catholic diocese of Phoenix has refused to marry a couple because the man is a quadriplegic unable to consummate the union, the church says. ("Church Refuses to Marry Couple," *Birmingham Post-Herald*, July 5, 1982, p. C10)

*12-19 André must use a pencil to dial a telephone, because his fingers won't fit the holes in the dial. ("A Giant Among Us," by Terry Todd, *Reader's Digest*, May 1982, p. 117)

12-20 The frequent claim that no true scientist can be a Bible-believing Christian or creation-ist is refuted by the fact that the greatest scientists of earlier generations *did* believe the Bible and in God as Creator. ("Two New Books Published by ICR Scientists," *Acts & Facts*, March 1982, p. 2)

12-21   Lamport finds a number of uses for the computer in his business, and while he was in the market for a brownstone co-op apartment, he fed into it all sorts of figures like yearly maintenance and tax-deductible operating expenses in order to determine the real cost of each piece of property—another confirmation of the axiom that computers have no intelligence of their own, since a machine with any brains would have taken one look at a collection of New York real-estate figures and typed out, "MOVE TO ST. PAUL." (*American Fried: Adventures of a Happy Eater*, by Calvin Trillin, pp. 84–85)

12-22   Because Indonesia is tropical, Indonesian cooks like bright colors. ("International Dish Is Judged Top Recipe," by Sue Scattergood, *Birmingham News*, January 18, 1984, p. 1D)

12-23   The misconception that because communists are atheists and secular humanists are atheists, therefore secular humanists must be communists, is prevalent. (Letter by Leonard R. Reid, Milwaukee, Wis., *Free Inquiry*, Winter 1983/84, p. 3)

12–24 William Burroughs interviewed by Susan Stanberg:

Burroughs:
I'm not Mr. Hearst.

Stanberg:
What do you mean?

Burroughs:
Well, you know his house-rule don't you?

Stanberg:
No.

Burroughs:
No one could mention death in his presence.

Stanberg:
William Randolph Hearst?

Burroughs:
Yes. If they mentioned death their luggage was outside in 5 minutes.

Stanberg:
Ha. Ha.

Burroughs:
That shows that he could never have been a writer.

Stanberg:
Why? What do you . . .?

Burroughs:
Can you imagine a writer who could never hear the word 'death' pronounced in his presence? I can't.

("All Things Considered," NPR, WBHM, February 10, 1984)

12-25 "God can see in this playhouse," Shelby said, pulling his hand away.

"No, he can't, Shelby," Matille said, sitting up and looking him hard in the eye. "God can't see through tin. This is a tin roof and God can't see through it." ("Summer, An Elegy," *In the Land of Dreamy Dreams*, by Ellen Gilchrist, p. 165)

12-26 Since leather is the skin of an animal, it can be cleaned with warm water and mild soap, just like your own. (*Things to Make with Leather: Techniques & Projects*, p. 33)

Section 13

Fallacies One

Argument from Authority
Two Wrongs Make a Right
Irrelevant Reason
Argument from Ignorance
Ambiguous Argument
Slippery Slope
Argument from Force

Introduction

Having presented two classes of maximally good arguments (that is, valid deductive arguments), in the remaining sections we discuss various types of arguments that are usually bad arguments—fallacies.

The named fallacies that are typically discussed in informal logic texts represent only some of the ways in which arguments can be bad—but they are the ones that are common enough that they have been given names. However, although 'fallacy' suggests a bad argument, there can be examples of some of the types of fallacies that are perfectly good arguments.

A further problem with fallacies is knowing how to classify them—which ones to consider together, which to treat as of different types. The grouping of fallacies chosen for Sections 13 through 16 conforms most closely with the categorization of fallacies found in some of the most popular informal logic texts.

To be fully explained, each fallacy needs a rather lengthy discussion, which is beyond what can be offered here. The summary descriptions in this introduction should be supplemented with a more full treatment from other sources.

This section contains examples of the following types of fallacies:

Argument from Authority

This is an argument where the reason given for a position is that some authority holds that position. Such arguments are satisfactory where the authority is a genuine authority on the topic in question and where the opinion of authorities on that topic is not divided. Often such arguments are bad arguments because the "authority" is not an authority on the topic in question or the "authority" is no authority at all but merely a "star" or "personality." Two special versions of the argument from authority are the *argument from popularity* and the *argument from traditional wisdom* where, respectively, the bulk of humankind or tradition is appealed to as the "authority." The exact opposite of the argument from popularity—what one might call '*the argument from exclusivity*'—attempts to argue for a conclusion on the basis that it is a position held by some select few. (Arguments from exclusivity are sometimes found in cigarette and liquor advertisments.) These special versions of the argument from authority are probably always bad arguments.

Two Wrongs Make a Right

This is an attempt to argue that some wrong is, in fact, not a wrong because someone (or something) else has committed the same act. Probably such arguments are always bad arguments. A special version of this fallacy is the *argument from common practice*—attempting to argue that something is not wrong because it is widespread.

Irrelevant Reason

The fallacy of irrelevant reason is an "argument" where the given "reasons" are irrelevant to the "conclusion." Any "argument" that has nil strength commits this fallacy.

Argument from Ignorance

A person who argues for some conclusion on the basis that there is no evidence against that conclusion is making an argument from ignorance. This argument comes very close to committing the fallacy of irrelevant reason.

Ambiguous Argument

An ambiguous argument is one where a faulty conclusion is reached because of some ambiguous expression in the premises of the argument. A special version of this argument is the *fallacy of stress*, where an ambiguity occurs because by stressing different words in a statement, it can be given different meanings.

Slippery Slope

Arguing that one event will lead to another, then to yet another, and so on in a chain reaction is called a slippery slope fallacy. Obviously, such arguments are sometimes satisfactory, sometimes not. Each claim that one event will lead to the next in the chain must be considered individually for its plausibility.

Argument from Force

This is an attempt to get a person to accept some conclusion or to do something by threatening dire consequences if he doesn't. A special version is the *argument from pity*, where the "dire consequences" are that someone (often the author of the argument) will be in piteous circumstances. Whereas such arguments obviously might motivate a person to do something, they don't provide good reasons (that is, reasons for doing that thing independently of the threat).

Two books that discuss most of the fallacies covered in Sections 13 through 15 are the following:

Howard Kahane, *Logic and Contemporary Rhetoric*, 4th ed. Ch. 2, 4

Patrick J. Hurley, *A Concise Introduction to Logic*, Ch. 3

Be aware that different authors might use different names for the same fallacy and different authors might give slightly different accounts of the fallacy of the same name.

Sections 13-16: Instructions

Most of the passages in the following sections contain illustrations of one or more fallacies. However, some are items discussing such fallacies.

Most of the examples are arguments, and it might be instructive to analyze and draw argument diagrams for some of these examples. However, the main exercise in the examples is the discussion of fallacies and a consequent evaluation of the argument.

1. Discuss whether any fallacies are committed in the passage. It is not sufficient to simply name some fallacy. Explain exactly in what way the example commits the fallacy.

2. Always examine a passage for more than one fallacy. A passage can commit two or more fallacies in two different ways: (a) because it contains two distinct problems and (b) because one type of fallacy is a subtype of another type of fallacy. (For example, all irrelevant reason fallacies are also examples of the fallacy of hasty conclusion—see Section 14. Because irrelevant reason is the more specific fallacy, it should be mentioned, where appropriate, rather than—or in addition to—the fallacy of hasty conclusion.)

3. If the passage is capable of more than one interpretation, discuss the passage on the interpretation you feel is most reasonable, but mention other possible interpretations. Sometimes passages are sufficiently unclear that conflicting interpretations are equally plausible.

4. Come to some overall assessment of the worth of argument. Remember that some examples of these types of "fallacies" can be good arguments.

A few of the exercises in the following sections are repeated in more than one section. Where this occurs, it is because the same exercise illustrates more than one fallacy.

Section 13: Exercises

13-1 FROM THE DESK OF JILL CLAYBURGH

Dear Friend,

As someone who has long been an ardent supporter of consumer rights, I am much impressed with the work of Dr. Michael Jacobson and his Center for Science in the Public Interest.

Supported primarily by private contributions and staffed by talented professionals and volunteers, this dynamic organization works continuously and effectively in defense of nutrition, health, and the welfare of all Americans.

Considering all the good that the Center has done during just ten years of existence, it's hard to imagine how anyone can refuse this tireless group a contribution of personal support.

I've joined. Won't you?

Sincerely,

Jill Clayburgh

(Note accompanying contribution-soliciting letter from Center for Science in the Public Interest, November 1983)

13-2 Tomorrow could also be the last day of the rest of your life—If you don't like thinking about safety, think where you might be without it. (Ad, *Nutshell*, Fall 1983, p. 96)

*13-3 Clinique believes in soap for faces. For the best reason in the world. Because *dermatologists* generally favor soap for daily facial cleansing and nobody knows more about what's good for skin then physicians dealing with skin. ("Why Soap?" in the pamphlet "What's So Different About Clinique Facial Soap?")

13-4 The best costs you less because moving is our business. (Ad for U-Haul, *Newsweek*, August 30, 1982, p. 43)

13-5 Tracy Austin: SATISFIED

Tracy Austin moves fast and travels light, so the compact, easy-to-use AE-1 is her ideal companion. For shooting sports action or recording travel memories, it satisfies her needs. In fact, since she first started using her AE-1, photography has become her favorite pastime. Next to tennis. Tracy Austin isn't alone. In the time since its introduction, more than one million Canon AE-1's have been bought in the United States and it's still going strong. Making it far and away the most successful camera of its type in history. A million satisfied customers must know something! (Ad for Canon cameras, *Newsweek*, May 4, 1981, p. 6)

13-6   DOG PROCLAIMS INNOCENCE BY TELEPATHY

Dean Goodman of Los Angeles was killed when his car plunged off a canyon road. His remains were not found for nineteen days. His German shepherd was with him; the dog was still alive when the man's body was found. Goodman's mother assumed that it was the dog, Prince, who had partially eaten the dead man's body, and she was determined to have the dog destroyed. But this gross injustice was narrowly averted when North Hollywood psychic Beatrice Lydecker interviewed the dog and found that Prince had in fact been wrongfully accused. "I have this ESP with animals," Mrs. Lydecker explained. "Prince had been traumatized by the accident. All Prince could talk about was his dead master." Coyotes and wild dogs, the German shepherd said, had eaten the body, despite Prince's valiant efforts to drive them off. The canine Hero's life was spared, owing to this timely information. A local police sargeant observed, "She says she got the information from the dog—and I've no evidence to dispute that." (*Skeptical Inquirer*, Winter 1978, p. 13, quoted in *Science and Unreason*, by Daisie and Michael Radner, p. 43. Reprinted by permission.)

13-7   If you fail to respond to guidance during the period of probation, you may be terminated. (*You & UAB: Handbook for Administrative, Professional and Support Personnel*, p. 31)

13-8   OWN THE BINOCULAR NASA CHOSE FOR APOLLO/SOYUZ! (Ad for Edmund Scientific Co., *Popular Mechanics*, July 1976, p. 133)

13-9   Jim Gillis, a senior philosophy major, and his partner Bob Poretto were told August 2 they could not use the word "saloon" in the title of their nightclub. . . .

A law put on the Alabama books in the 1930s prohibits the use of the words "bar, buffet, or saloon" in the name of businesses that serve alcohol. . . .

"It's also against the law to use the words 'beer, whiskey, wine and ale' on your signs, and other places are breaking that law," he [Gillis] said. ("Saloon Fighting for Right to Keep Name," by Charlie Ingram, *Kaleidoscope*, September 30, 1983, p. 2)

13-10   TODAY'S WEATHER REPORT

I was somewhat dismayed by your choice of words in describing Willard Scott of NBC's "Today" show as a "meteorologist" and "jocular climatologist" (Newsmakers, Sept. 5). Neither title applies to Scott—though he may be jocular. As a member of the American Meteorological Society and the National Weather Association, I would like to point out that a meteorologist or climatologist is someone who has completed a professional course of study or made some equivalent, accredited contribution to the field. Unfortunately, people are frequently confused as to who's a meteorologist and who's not, and those of us who are doing our best to provide reliable forecasts suffer because of it.—Willard Watts, Lafayette, Ind. ("Letters," *Newsweek*, October 3, 1983, pp. 12, 14)

*13–11 I have always thought that anyone who sacrifices stuffing power by using chopsticks in a Chinese restaurant must be demented. I would use a tablespoon if I thought I could get away with it, but I know that the people I tend to share my Chinatown meals with, terrified that I would polish off the twice-fried pork before they had a chance to say "Pass the bean curd," would start using tablespoons themselves, and sooner or later we would be off on an escalating instruments race that might end with soup ladles or dory-bailers. (*American Fried: Adventures of a Happy Eater*, by Calvin Trillin, p. 61)

13–12 Touching this pylon means instant death. Anyone doing so will be subject to prosecution. (Notice on electricity pylon in Sussex, England)

13–13 "The quality of Smirnoff is something to sing about. Its value calls for encores."—Diahann Carroll, singer and actress (Ad for Smirnoff vodka, *Gentlemen's Quarterly*, September 1983, inside front cover)

13–14 Authoritative voice: FARM BUREAU IS BETTER THAN GOLD.

Weak voice: Better than Gold?

Authoritative voice: *YES*, BETTER THAN GOLD!

(Radio commercial, WAPI, Birmingham, Alabama, Summer 1980)

13–15 The smooth, mellow taste of Early Times Kentucky Whisky has been a part of the good life since 1860.

The taste and tradition continue. (Ad for Early Times Kentucky Whisky, *Newsweek*, October 24, 1983, p. 101)

13–16 One of every 500 persons alive today is possessed by the devil, says a respected senior cleric of the Church of England. ("Demons Taking Over Says Top Exorcist," *Globe*, August 16, 1983, p. 2)

13–17 "YOU CAN FEEL IT WHEN YOU DRIVE"—Lee Trevino.

"I can feel new Bridgestone SuperFiller radials when I stop, start, or corner . . . when I drive.

"I'm certainly not the first to tell you that the grip is important when you drive.

"Put the advanced technology of Bridgestone SuperFiller radials between you and the road. You can feel it when you drive." (Ad for Bridgestone tires, *Newsweek*, August 31, 1981, p. 32)

13–18 Administration officials have warned repeatedly, as Reagan did again Thursday, that unless Muammar Khadafy is stopped in Chad, he will seek to destabilize all of North Africa. ("U.S. Frustrated with France, but Won't Intervene in Chad," *Birmingham News*, August 12, 1983, p. 1A)

13-19   "Folonari Soave. Clean, Crisp . . . one of the best buys."—Terry Robards, Wine Critic, *New York Times* (9/24/80) (Ad for Folonari, *Time*, November 16, 1981, p. 106)

13-20   HINKLE ROOFING

                          "SYNONYMOUS WITH ROOFING"

                                  SINCE 1908
         (Ad for Hinkle Roofing, *Greater Birmingham Yellow Pages*, August 1983, p. 742)

*13-21   Just before we left, we finally got to the question that had been bothering us for days. If it was true that it [planting by the signs of the moon] *did* work, then *why*? Why did it work? Margaret supplied an answer—"Well, it must have been in th' plan when th' world was made. Because you know in Ecclesiastes it says, 'There's a time for everything. A time to be born and a time to die. A time to plant and a time to harvest.' That's God's book, you know, so that's the reason." (*The Foxfire Book*, ed. Eliot Wigginton, pp. 224–225)

13-22   PROTESTANTS VOW VIGILANTE ACTION

         Belfast, Northern Ireland (AP)—Protestant leaders, denouncing British pleas to keep calm after the assassination of a Protestant member of Parliament, announced today they will set up vigilante groups if Britain does not crack down on the Irish Republican Army.
              He [James Molyneaux] told a news conference that unless Britain meets an ultimatum to "mobilize the community to protect life and property" Protestants will do it themselves. (*Birmingham News*, November 16, 1981, p. 4A)

13-23   In 1980, the Domestic Foreign Missionary Society, a stockholder in U.S. Steel Corp., proposed that the corporation have its South African subsidiaries subscribe to the Sullivan Principles or sell these subsidiaries. One of the reasons they gave in support of the proposal was that:
              More than 115 major United States Corporations, including IBM, Exxon, Ford, General Motors, Mobil, General Electric, Aramco Steel, Kennecott Copper, Phelps Dodge, and Union Carbide, have subscribed to the six "Sullivan Principles" which set forth minimum desegregation and fair employment standards for American corporations operating in South Africa.
         (*U.S. Steel Corporation, Notice of Annual Meeting*, 1980, p. 14)

13-24   A little girl shouldn't have to beg for food.
              But Nita must.
              Her frail mother, who spends all day in the marketplace peddling straw mats, can't sell enough to feed Nita and her two younger brothers.
              For $15 a month through our sponsorship program, you can help a child like Nita.
         (Ad for Children, Inc., *Newsweek*, February 16, 1981, p. 12)

13-25 FTC MAKES EXAMPLE OF GAS-GADGET PROMOTERS

The G-R Valve is a little plastic gizmo that's supposed to save gasoline. . . . The G-R Valve has been sold nationwide with television, print, and direct-mail ads featuring effusive endorsements by ex-astronaut Gordon Cooper. The Federal Trade Commission has taken vigorous action on the G-R Valve. . . .

The agreement reached with Cooper reflects the FTC's position that celebrity endorsers should assume some responsibility for what they say in advertisements . . . The agreement not only prohibits the ex-astronaut's claims for the product, but also forbids Cooper from representing himself as an expert in fields in which he lacks the necessary qualifications. (*Consumer Reports*, February 1980, p. 112)

*13-26 The Moral Majority's Rev. Jerry Falwell relies more peculiarly on Christian authority. He claims that Jesus Christ favored the death penalty. On the Cross, Falwell says, He could have spoken up: "If ever there was a platform for our Lord to condemn capital punishment, that was it. He did not." ("An Eye for an Eye," by Kurt Andersen, *Time*, January 24, 1983, p. 36)

13-27 BAD WEATHER CAUSED BY RUSSIANS

While most scientists are still studying the causes for the two successive harsh winters to hit North America, researcher George Stone believes he has found the answer. Stone, who claims to be a geologist and weather expert, and to have worked secretly with the CIA, says that the abnormally cold weather was probably caused by the Soviet Cosmos satellite which crashed early this year in northern Canada. "I feel that satellite may well have been controlling our weather all along the East Coast, and probably other parts of the country," he told the tabloid *The Star*. "The satellite that crashed in Canada in January was in just the right position to control our weather all along the East Coast, where the snowstorms hit . . . I admit I have no hard evidence, but then there is no negative evidence either. (*Skeptical Inquirer*, Fall 1978, p. 15, quoted in *Science and Unreason*, by Daisie and Michael Radner, p. 83. Reprinted by permission.)

13-28 Now the serpent was more subtle than any other wild creature that the Lord God had made. He said to the woman, "Did God say, 'You shall not eat of any tree of the garden'?" And the woman said to the serpent, "We may eat of the fruit of the trees of the garden; but God said, 'You shall not eat of the fruit of the tree which is in the midst of the garden, neither shall you touch it, lest you die.' " (*Gen. 3: 1-3*)

13-29 "Being active can drain a man's body of zinc—a metal 'more precious than gold' for good health." Dan Gable, Olympic Wrestling Champion Coach of 1980 U.S. Olympic Wrestling Team . . . "That's why I make sure our wrestling team takes Z-BEC. It's rich in zinc—a metal 'more precious than gold' for helping a man stay in shape." (Ad for Z-BEC, *Newsweek*, May 4, 1981, p. 39)

13–30   Soike still won't go out on the Fourth of July because that was the day the rocket nearly killed him in Vietnam. ("When Charlie Came Home," by Peter Goldman, *Reader's Digest*, May 1982, pp. 126–127)

13–31   AMERICA'S FIRST NAME FOR HAM.
More than 50 years ago, Hormel introduced America's first ham in a can, a milestone in meat convenience. Since then, we have never stopped working to increase our skills in ham-making. . . . to preserve old-fashioned quality and flavor while pioneering new ham products for today's families . . . and to truly merit the title we've been given: America's first name in ham. (Ad for Hormel, *Reader's Digest*, December 1980, p. 118)

13–32   OUR POINT . . . CAN MAKE YOUR POINT . . . PRECISELY.

Want to be precise and to the point?

Try an Ultra Fine Flair pen.

You see, Ultra Fine has a precision point that delivers an incredibly smooth line of vivid Flair ink. So everything you write will be precise and to the point.

Look for Ultra Fine and refillable Ultra Fine where Flair pens are sold. (Ad for Flair pens, *Reader's Digest*, May 1982, p. 51)

13–33   Voted "most qualified" by 96% (9/15/80) B'ham Bar Association. Let's keep Judge W. C. Zanaty, Jr., Circuit Court—Democrat. (Billboard ad, Birmingham, Alabama, October 1980)

13–34   Old Grand-Dad still makes that Bourbon much as we did 100 years ago. (Ad for Old Grand-Dad bourbon, *Newsweek*, October 31, 1983, back cover)

13–35   The idea for the investigation grew out of a hearing earlier this year for a restaurant owner accused of selling alcohol to minors, Gray said. The restaurant owner said he felt he was being singled out unfairly, and charged that employees in ABC stores also were selling to minors, Gray said. ("47 ABC Employees Accused of Selling Alcohol to Minors," by William Bunch, *Birmingham News*, November 15, 1983, p. 1A)

13–36   CRACKER JACK

Since 1871, we've popped more popcorn than anyone. (Ad for Cracker Jack, *Good Housekeeping*, September 1983, p. 192)

13–37   "As a member of the queen's Privy Council and as a Knight—my correct title is the Right Honorable Sir Eric Gairy—I should not be harassed in my own country," he declared. "They must understand that I control the majority of this island. If I want to retaliate, it could be a tough time." ("Gairy Flexes His Musclemen," by Edward Cody, *Washington Post* section, *Manchester Guardian Weekly*, February 12, 1984, p. 15)

13-38 In a cartoon showing a school bus (labeled "National Bussing") hanging over a cliff-edge ready to topple onto a school-house, a man representing the Justice Department says to a local school official, referring to the bus, "Remember, we've got it hanging over your head at all times—if you don't do as we think you should." (*Birmingham News*, November 20, 1980, p. 7A)

13-39 Dialogue from a Drabble cartoon strip:

Frame 1—Drabble:
"Say, Wendy, after work, would you like to go to a movie with me?"

Frame 2—Wendy:
"Go to a movie with you?"

Frame 3—Wendy:
"I'd rather do time in a Turkish jail."

Frame 4—Drabble:
"How about bowling?"

(*Birmingham News*, November 27, 1977, p. 6B)

Section 14

Fallacies Two

Ad Hominem Argument
Provincialism
Tokenism
Hasty Conclusion
Questionable Classification
Questionable Analogy
Questionable Cause
Loaded Phrase or Question

Introduction

Refer to the Introduction to Section 13 for general comments on fallacies and references to books with more full discussion of fallacies.

The fallacies illustrated in the examples of this section are as follows:

Ad Hominem Argument

The ad hominem argument is an attempt to argue against a position by citing someone who holds that position and making an "attack" on that person, rather than on the position espoused by the person. If the ad hominem argument is construed as an argument that the position espoused by the person is false, it is always a bad argument. If its conclusion is merely that one has no reason for accepting the position espoused, the argument can be good depending on the nature of the "attack" on the person. (It is good, for instance, if the "attack" is that the person is a liar or that the person is an interested party in the subject at hand.) Most often ad hominem arguments are bad arguments because the "attack" on the person is usually totally irrelevant to the person's espoused position. Very often the conclusions of ad hominem arguments are merely insinuated, not stated—which is probably an indication that the author recognizes the argument is weak. In the *guilt by association version* of the ad hominem argument, the "attack" on the person is that he or she is associated with some generally disapproved-of group.

Fallacy of Provincialism

This argument is that some view or practice is superior or correct merely because it is familiar or accepted locally.

Fallacy of Tokenism

The tokenism fallacy occurs when merely token efforts are made to right some wrong when a person is charged with wrongdoing.

Fallacy of Hasty Conclusion

This is jumping to a conclusion on the basis of insufficient evidence. Clearly, any argument that has weak or nil strength commits this fallacy. Charging this fallacy amounts to little more than claiming that the argument is a bad argument.

Fallacy of Questionable Classification

The argument of this fallacy arrives at some conclusion on the basis of incorrectly classifying together things that should be classified separately.

Fallacy of Questionable Analogy

Arriving at some conclusion on the basis of incorrectly drawing an analogy between two situations that are not sufficiently analogous is called questionable analogy. Because to draw an analogy between two situations is to claim that those situations share some features, and because this is to classify the two situations together, often when a charge of questionable analogy is appropriate it is equally appropriate to charge questionable classification, and vice versa.

Fallacy of Questionable Cause

The questionable cause fallacy is arguing to the conclusion that one event is the cause of another when there is insufficient evidence for such a causal relation. The most usual form of this fallacy is arguing that one thing causes another simply on the evidence that the two things always occur together.

Fallacy of Loaded Phrases (or Questions)

This fallacy consists in making an assertion (or asking a question) that makes an assumption that might not be justified. (For example, saying 'She has never been divorced' or asking 'Have you ever been divorced?' would normally be taken to assume that the person in question has been married.)

For instructions for doing the following exercises, refer to the instructions in Section 13.

Section 14: Exercises

14–1 No one has done more for the cause of ancient astronauts than Erich von Daniken, a former hotel manager from Switzerland. (*Science and Unreason*, by Daisie and Michael Radner, p. 3)

14–2 It is widely believed that in the summer rich people leave New York to go to Southampton because the weather is cooler there. This is not true. What actually happens is that in the summer the cooler weather leaves New York and goes to Southampton because it doesn't want to stay in New York with a lot of underpaid writers and Puerto Ricans. ("Good Weather and Its Propensity to Frequent the Better Neighborhoods," *Metropolitan Life*, by Fran Lebowitz, p. 96)

14–3 Virtually everyone who has worked or dealt with Ronald Reagan in Hollywood describes him as warm, friendly, decent, intelligent and industrious. Virtually no one describes him as erudite, scholarly, academic, profound, creative or intellectual.

With his set of character traits, it is probable that Reagan's Presidency will turn out to be only as good as the men he has chosen to advise him.

Two of these are Caspar Weinberger, an adroit, tough, calculating master of infighting who runs the Pentagon for Reagan; and Gen. Alexander Haig who violates one of this country's cherished traditions—the noninvolvement of a military officer with partisan politics—and has the job of Secretary of State to show for it.

[The article goes on to discuss Haig's support of El Salvador, and Weinberger's advocacy of the MX and the B-1.] ("Reagan's Advisors: An Assessment," *Parade*, November 1, 1982, p. 3)

14–4 In fact there was only one species on the planet [Earth] more intelligent than dolphins, and they spent a lot of their time in behavioral research laboratories running round inside wheels and conducting frighteningly elegant and subtle experiments on man. The fact that once again man completely misinterpreted this relationship was entirely according to these creatures' plans. (*The Hitchhiker's Guide to the Galaxy*, by Douglas Adams, pp. 156–157)

14–5 The Victorian notion that acne was somehow related to teen-age sexual habits has long been discarded. But one can see why the connection was made. The same adolescent flood of hormones that transforms children into adults also awakens the sebaceous glands—small glands that underlie all areas of the skin except the palms and soles. Those glands grow larger and begin secreting a complex mixture of oils called sebum.

Sebum has been called "the fuel of the acne flame." People with acne tend to produce more sebum, on average, than those without acne. Men generally secrete more sebum and tend to get more severe acne than women. ("How Acne Develops," *Consumer Reports*, August 1981, p. 472)

14-6 Kelly Segraves, who brought suit in California [to have the teaching of "creation science" included in the school curriculum] on behalf of his son, has written many textbooks, heavy in creationism, which are published and printed by the organization he heads. The adoption of textbooks by school systems can involve tremendous profits for the publishers and significant royalties for the authors. Before we become swayed by the silver tongues of some of these "Moral" Majority, "born again" spokesmen who want to tell us how to live, what to read and what to teach in our schools, a check on their incomes and investments might be in order. ("Evolution Argument Ignores Natural Science Goals," by Jim Hawk, *Kaleidoscope*, August 2, 1983, p. 5)

14-7 Sentiment for repeal began to be expressed in influental circles. Testifying before a Senate Judiciary Committee, Samuel Gompers, President of the American Federation of Labor, said, "Depriving the American Workingman of his glass of beer tends to promote industrial unrest and discontent . . . Such things as this arbitrary legislation breeds Bolshevism." (A few years earlier it had been the Anti-Saloon League which brandished this familiar bugaboo: "Bolshevism flourishes in wet soil. Failure to enforce Prohibition in Russia was followed by Bolshevism.") (*Eating in America: A History*, by Waverley Root and Richard de Rochemont, p. 399)

*14-8 One of every 500 persons alive today is possessed by the devil, says a respected senior cleric of the Church of England.

"Possession once was almost wiped out in the Christian countries but now it's very much with us again," declares the Very Rev. Philip Pare, exorcist for the Oxford diocese for 10 years. . . .

Pare attributes the recent increase in demonic activity to the decline in the practice of baptism. "For almost 1,000 years nearly everyone in this country [England] was baptized," he says. "Today the figure is somewhere under 70 per cent.

"Baptism is not a sure preventive, but it certainly helps. You can think of it as a sort of spiritual vaccination." ("Demons Taking Over Says Top Exorcist," *Globe*, August 16, 1983, p. 2)

14-9 The ECS therapy used for mentally disturbed humans may be compared with the kicking of a recalcitrant machine: both imply a profound ignorance of the underlying mechanism, but they sometimes work. (*The Metaphorical Brain*, by Michael A. Arbib, p. 68)

14-10 In 1913 an Aurora, Illinois, resident named Marshall B. Gardner—he was in charge of maintenance of machinery for a large corset company—published privately a small book titled *Journey to the Earth's Interior*. It described a hollow earth . . . Only the outer shell, he insisted, is known to exist. It is 800 miles thick. Inside the hollow, a sun, 600 miles in diameter, gives perpetual daylight to the interior. There are openings at both poles, each 1,400 miles across. (*Fads and Fallacies: In the Name of Science*, by Martin Gardner, p. 21)

*14–11 BEAUTY SECRET

When you're studying late, your mind often gets blurry and you feel you can't cram another fact into your tired brain. Take a fifteen-minute break to clear your head. Put on quiet music and stretch like a lazy cat to loosen up. And smooth Oil of Olay Beauty Fluid over your face for a refreshing pickup. Don't you feel better already? (Ad for Oil of Olay, *Nutshell*, Fall 1981, p. 44)

14–12 Miss America Debra Sue Moffett recently went to great lengths to explain the difference between beauty pageants. She called the Miss U.S.A. competition "just a skin show." However her remarks must be taken with a grain of salt. The 26-year-old American beauty has confirmed that she twice failed to win the title of Miss U.S.A. She twice was runner-up in Miss U.S.A. preliminaries in Texas. On Tuesday, while appearing at the opening of a shopping mall in Maryville, Tenn., she told reporters that Miss U.S.A. contestants were "judged strictly on outward appearance." For those who thought the same standards apply to the Miss America Contest, Miss Moffett set the record straight: "The program I represent has more depth to it." For further clarification she said "Miss America is like the girl who lives next door. Miss U.S.A. looks like the girl you wish lived next door." ("Beauty Only Skin Deep?" by Kasey Jones, *Birmingham Post-Herald*, March 4, 1983, p. A11. Reprinted by permission)

14–13 Washington—Most Americans think President Reagan is a very nice guy, but aides fear that flyspecks are beginning to mar that image.

   Most recently, his top assistants winced at the sharp edge to the president's rhetoric in speeches made at midweek in Cheyenne, Wyo., Albuquerque, N.M., and Los Angeles ... Quite indiscriminately, he denounced congressional critics of the budget as "sob sisters." ("Aides Feel Reagan Hurt 'Mr. Nice Guy' Image," by Loye Miller, Jr., *Birmingham News*, March 7, 1982, p. 25A)

14–14 The children who had imaginary companions differed sharply from the rest: they were less aggressive and more cooperative; they smiled more; they showed a greater ability to concentrate; they were seldom bored; and their language was richer and more advanced, especially among the boys.

   "For example, they use the future tense more when they speak, and also more adverbs and adjectives," Dorothy Singer points out. "The others seem limited to the present tense and to simple commands: 'Do this, do that.' "

   Another major difference was that the children with imaginary playmates watched far less television—only half as many hours per week. And even when they did watch the screen, their choice of programs was quite different; they were not interested in cartoons and violent shows that the other group preferred.

"All the constructive characteristics seem to be correlated with imaginary playmates in our children," says Dorothy Singer. ("Invisible Playmates," by Maya Pines, *Psychology Today*, September 1978, p. 38. Reprinted by permission)

14-15   Sports is the toy department of human life. (Jimmy Cannon, quoted by Howard Cosell, "Quotable Quotes," *Reader's Digest*, May 1982, inside front cover)

14-16   Erich von Daniken, whose distinctions include a jail term in his native Switzerland for embezzlement, widely popularized the notion that no mere human beings could have constructed the pyramids of Egypt, the statues of Easter Island, and other feats of preindustrial engineering. They must, therefore, have been made by extraterrestrial visitors. ("Little Green Men from Afar," by L. Sprague de Camp, *Humanist*, July/August 1976, pp. 6–7)

14-17   I'll admit that I was a little skeptical when I first heard of glucomannan capsules. Glucomannan, a 100% natural high dietary fibre, is the scientific name for Super-Mannan. However, I decided to check this product out carefully. They're made from the rare Konjac root (found only in a few limited areas of Japan)—and I know that people in Japan and the Orient aren't plagued by the problem of overweight, as are far too many Americans. (Ad for Super-Mannan by Jack LaLanne, *Parade*, July 4, 1982, p. 20)

14-18   More serious is Duncan's snide attempt to play down the incidence of torture in Iran. Dismissing the Amnesty researcher on Iran as a "well-meaning woman from Hampstead" this rather less well-meaning man from Hampstead (for there indeed does our author reside) criticizes her for not carrying out her investigations in Iran. He omits to tell us that Amnesty was for years banned by the Shah from doing so. ("Helping Hands," a review by Fred Halliday of *Money Rush*, by Andrew Duncan, *Manchester Guardian Weekly*, Februrary 25, 1979, p. 20)

14-19   The humanistic assumption that significant truth can be discovered apart from conversion to Christ is, in Schaeffer's view, the source of the despair he sees reflected in contemporary culture.

Such generalizations are typical of Schaeffer, whose method of argument is to capsulize complex thinkers such as Kant and Kierkegaard in a paragraph or two in order to dismiss them. In his most ambitious book, "How Shall We Then Live?" Schaeffer ranges through the whole of Western Civilization without a single supporting footnote. . . .

Adds Wheaton historian Mark Noll: "The danger is that people will take him for a scholar, which he is not. Evangelical historians are especially bothered by his simplified myth of America's Christian past." ("Guru of Fundamentalism," by Kenneth L. Woodward, *Newsweek*, November 1, 1982, p. 88)

14-20

> THE FAMILY THAT PRAYS TOGETHER STAYS TOGETHER

(Bumper sticker)

14–21   Creationists tend to appeal to authority—to neat, easy solutions to complex questions. Such arguments tend to be attractive to the frustrated, the needful, and the alienated. ("Science and Evolution in the Public Eye," by Laurie R. Godfrey, in *Paranormal Borderlands of Science*, ed. Kendrick Frazier, pp. 382–383)

14–22   DIET WITH MEAT SUPERIOR, STUDY SAYS

Holding to a diet containing meat will result in improved work productivity, less cheating, and few psychological and physical problems for the dieter, according to a recent study.

Writing in *Food and Nutrition News*, a National Live Stock and Meat Board publication, Maria Simonson compared three groups of dieters.

The 227 subjects with weight problems were divided thusly:

— Group one ate a self-designed vegetarian diet.
— Group two ate a vegetarian diet individually designed by a registered dietician.
— Group three ate a balanced, low calorie diet containing meat, fish, dairy products, fruits, cereals and vegetables.

Simonson, an assistant professor at the Johns Hopkins School of Medicine, noted that while the vegetarian groups shed weight a little faster, the meat eaters with the balanced diet had fewer dropouts, lower stress levels, reported no feelings of hunger, and had increased work efficiency by 13 per cent. (*Birmingham News*, May 30, 1982, p. 2G. Reprinted by permission)

14–23   Joseph Smith reportedly used a "seer stone" to translate the *Book of Mormon* from gold plates. Four years earlier he had attempted to use such a stone to look for buried treasure. At that time, he was brought to trial as a "glass-looker" and an imposter and was convicted of disorderly conduct. ("Joseph Smith and the Book of Mormon," by George D. Smith, *Free Inquiry*, Winter 1983/84, p. 21)

14–24   More than six per cent of the inmates of San Quentin give their occupation as cook (laborers form the largest group and cooks the second largest); but male cooks compose less than two-tenths of one per cent of the total U.S. population, according to the 1930 census.

I would like to know to what type of crime cooks are peculiarly given. I have heard it said by men who have been much up and down in the world that cooks as a class are irascible men, with the instincts of dictators. It is an interesting speculation: does the profession attract men of a certain character, or are nerves and tempers shattered by the life they lead? Or does the emotional effect result from a physical deterioration of stomach and liver through too much tasting of their own cooking?

Just what, in brief, is the moral hazard involved in being a cook? (David Lamson, excerpted from *We Who Are About to Die*. Copyright 1935 Charles Scribner's Sons; copyright renewed 1963 David Lamson. Used by permission of Charles Scribner's Sons.)

14-25   When a company hires an accountant to keep the books, the first thing that he does is announce that he has so much work to do on the overall direction of the company's financial policy that he needs to hire a junior accountant to keep the books. Something similar happens with spies. A country sets up an intelligence service to find out how many tanks its neighbor has and where they are kept, and before you can say M15 the intelligence service announces that it is so busy spying on subversive elements at home that a separate service is needed to deal with military intelligence. (*Triple*, by Ken Follett, p. 45)

14-26   Incest taboos are among the universals of human social behavior. The avoidance of sexual intercourse between brothers and sisters and between parents and their offspring is everywhere achieved by cultural sanctions. But at least with brother-sister taboo, there exists a far deeper, less rational form of enforcement: a sexual aversion automatically develops between persons who have lived together when one or all grew to the age of six.

What advantage do the incest taboos confer? A favored explanation amongst anthropologists is that the taboos preserve the integrity of the family by avoiding the confusion in roles that would result from incestuous sex. Another . . . is that it facilitates the exchange of women during bargaining between social groups. Sisters and daughters, in this view, are not used for mating but to gain power.

In contrast, the prevailing sociobiological explanation regards family integration and bridal bargaining as byproducts or at most as secondary contributing factors. It identifies a deeper, more urgent cause, the heavy physiological penalty imposed by inbreeding. Several studies by human geneticists have demonstrated that even a moderate amount of inbreeding results in children who are diminished in overall body size, muscular coordination, and academic performance. ("The Nature of Human Nature," *New Scientist*, October 5, 1978, p. 20. Reprinted by permission)

14-27   Defense lawyers quickly conceded that their clients had taken the money. They argued, however, that none of their clients had done anything in return. The defense hopes to fix the blame on a convicted swindler named Melvin Weinberg, who worked with the FBI during Abscam and appears in the videotapes. The lawyers insist that Weinberg conned the defendants into bragging in front of the cameras and thinking that they could keep the cash with no strings attached. ("Abscam Presents: Take the Money . . .," *Newsweek*, August 25, 1980, p. 52)

14-28   Claudia Jacobs, a teacher of children in the Cambridge (Massachusetts) school system termed "learning disabled," has told me that well over half of the children she sees for tutorials are hyperactive, as well as learning disabled and that most of the children that she sees are boys. Naturally, this brings up the question as to whether the hyperactivity and learning problems are causally related. Is the child hyperactive because he has specific learning problems? Does he have specific learning problems because he is so active that he does not concentrate in school? Or, is it that the hyperactivity and learning problems are causally unrelated, but occur together? ("Hyperactive Children and the Drug Paradox," *New Scientist*, November 2, 1978, p. 350)

14–29 I am not among those people who have difficulty eating on airplanes because of anxieties connected with flying. As someone who travels constantly in the course of business, I naturally have no fears or superstitions brought on by being in an airplane; years ago, I discovered that I could keep the plane I was flying on from crashing by refusing to adjust my watch to the new time zone until we were on the ground, and I have used that method ever since. ("Fly Frills to Miami," *Alice, Let's Eat: Further Adventures of a Happy Eater*, by Calvin Trillin, p. 51)

14–30 Citizens for Fairness in Education is an organization based in Anderson, South Carolina, formed by Paul Ellwanger, a respiratory therapist who is trained in neither law nor science. Mr. Ellwanger is of the opinion that evolution is the forerunner of many social ills, including Nazism, racism, and abortion. (From the Memorandum Opinion by Judge William R. Overton, in McLean v. Arkansas Board of Education, reprinted in *Evolution, Morality, and the Meaning of Life*, by Jeffrie G. Murphy, p. 123)

*14–31 Gene Hill: "Training a dog isn't as complicated as training a wife, but the process is similar and the results we are looking for are about the same. We pick one from a litter, not quite sure of what we're getting, try to make friends with it right at first, and then spend a lot of time with it in the early stages so we can get to know how the other thinks. In training, this period is called yard work; in marriage, it's called a honeymoon. Both are noteworthy for causing tears." (*New Woman*, February 1982, p. 12)

14–32 Even when freshly washed and relieved of all obvious confections, children tend to be sticky. One can only assume that this has something to do with not smoking enough. ("Children: Pro or Con?" *Metropolitan Life*, by Fran Lebowitz, p. 34)

*14–33 The courtroom battle continued Saturday between John Sidote, the state's star witness in the murder trial of California feminist Ginny Foat, 42, and defense attorney Robert Glass.

The battle was joined on Friday, when Glass began his cross-examination, which lasted for four hours.

There were repeated clashes as Glass sought to characterize Sidote as a liar and a loser who is trying to gain parole from prison by cooperating with the state to convict his former wife.

Glass accused Sidote, 45, of lying at his 1967 trial in California for the shooting death of a patron of a bar that Sidote and Foat owned in Torrance, California . . .

Sidote is a witness with a past that casts a shadow on his veracity.

In addition to his involuntary manslaughter conviction for the California killing, he is serving a 25-year prison term in Nevada for manslaughter and robbery. ("Feminist's

Accuser Grilled in Death Trial," by Paul Galloway, *Birmingham News*, November 13, 1983, p. 7A. Reprinted by permission)

14-34 Watt told the group, "All of our wealth comes directly or indirectly from the land, whether that wealth is precious metals, grain, livestock, fibre or synthetics.

"If we are to have a future we must manage the land for the benefit of ourselves and our children yet to come."

And, repeating the policy that brought so much criticism during his three years as interior secretary, Watt said this means opening up federal lands to more development. ("Watt Says, 'Fun to Be Citizen,' " *Birmingham News*, November 9, 1983, p. 12A)

14-35 There is a natural affinity between a used-car salesman and a Congressman. Neither one wants you to know what's under the hood.

For this reason there was nothing surprising about Congress's rejection of Federal rules that would have forced used-car dealers to tell their customers about serious defects in their merchandise. . . .

Put yourself in your Congressman's shoes. One of these days he is going to be out of office. Defeated, old, tired, 120,000 miles on his smile and two pistons cracked in his best joke. They're going to put him out on the used-Congressman lot.

Does he want to have a sticker on him stating that he gets only eight miles on a gallon of bourbon? That his rip-roaring anti-Communist speech hasn't had an overhaul since 1969? That his generator is so decomposed it hasn't sparked a fresh thought in 15 years? ("Barnum Lives On," *The Rescue of Miss Yaskell and Other Pipe Dreams*, by Russell Baker, pp. 219–220)

14-36 From a Sam and Silo cartoon strip:

Frame 1—
A cat asleep on the sheriff's desk. The phone begins to ring.

Frame 2—
As the phone rings "Rinng, rinng . . .," the cat purrs back "Meow? Meow? . . ."

Frame 3—
The phone having stopped ringing, the cat says: "If you make as much noise as they do, pretty soon they give up."

(*Huntsville Times*, March 31, 1982)

Section 15

Fallacies Three

Suppressed Evidence
Questionable Premise
Straw Man
False Dilemma
Begging the Question
Inconsistency
Red Herring

Introduction

A general introduction to fallacies and references to texts that describe falla-cies in more detail are given in the Introduction to Section 13.

The fallacies illustrated by examples in this section are as follows:

Fallacy of Suppressed Evidence

This is the situation where widely available evidence (which there is good reason to suspect was known by the author) is omitted from an argument in order that a case can be made for some conclusion.

Questionable Premise

This fallacy describes an argument where there is strong reason for doubting the truth of one of its premises.

Straw Man Fallacy

The straw man fallacy attempts to give the impression that the person has ar-gued for a strong conclusion when, in fact, one has only argued for some weaker, but related, conclusion.

Fallacy of False Dilemma

In a false dilemma fallacy, a person presents in the premises of an argument two (or more) alternatives as if they were the only alternatives when, in fact, there are other possibilities.

Begging the Question

Making an assumption in the premises of an argument that is equally or more contentious than the conclusion a person is trying to establish is called begging the question. This fault in argumentation is similar to *circularity* (often the two names are used interchangeably). A person is said to be arguing circularly (or in a circle) when, if asked for his reasons for accepting the premises in an argument, he mentions the conclusion of the argument.

Inconsistency

Inconsistency is making two (or more) claims in an argument that can't both (all) be true together.

Red Herring (or *Evading the Issue*)

A red herring argument attempts to lead the topic from the subject matter at hand to some different, but usually related, topic. Red herring is, of course, part of the art of politics, and is often used to lead a conversation or interview away from topics that are difficult or embarrassing for the respondent to topics that are easy and safe. Skillful use of red herring demands that the transition to the new topic is not readily detected. Thus in a good red herring the topic the conversation is led to is usually related to the topic issue. For this reason straw man and red herring are often similar and/or found together. (Begging the question and evading the issue are quite different fallacies. Note the differences, as many people confuse the two.)

For instructions for doing the following exercises, refer to the instructions in Section 13.

Section 15: Exercises

*15–1 Magic 96—where we're halfway through ten songs in a row without interruption. (Announcer on WMJJ, Birmingham, Alabama, November 17, 1983)

15–2 CAMPBELL'S SOUP IS GOOD FOOD

In a recent study of government data, university researchers found that soup can play a significant part in a healthy, well-balanced diet. And a single serving of Campbell's Soup provides a variety of important nutrients.

Take Campbell's Bean with Bacon Soup. Calorie for calorie, it's more nutritionally balanced than an apple. Besides supplying major nutrients like vitamin A, it also contains several "trace elements" which the body needs in small but essential amounts to function properly.

And soup doesn't just outshine an apple. There really aren't many other foods that can match it for overall nutritional variety. (Ad for Campbell's soup, *Time*, March 7, 1983, p. 35)

15–3 On a tour of Yellowstone, Watt told reporters that he was being misrepresented in the press and that he had no intention of clearcutting, mining, or drilling within parks. This can hardly be taken as concession or a sign of good faith, however, because the activities he disowned are illegal in parks anyway.

But when a reporter asked Watt what he planned to do about threats from outside the parks, Watt simply smiled and replied, "It's a nice day. Let's enjoy the park." ("Geothermal Energy: Trouble Brews for the National Parks," by Bruce Hamilton, *Sierra*, July/August 1983, pp. 25–26)

15–4 I'm a terrible sleeper—Ronnie's good—and, especially after traveling, my timeclock is all mixed up, which makes me hungry when I'm not supposed to be.

My solution is to eat a banana when I wake up starved. I don't like to eat apples because that might wake my husband. ("One Non-Stop Day in My Whirlwind Life," by Nancy Reagan talking to reporter James Danziger, *Star*, June 29, 1982, p. 9)

15–5 When [he] stood in the well of the house to hear judgment . . . Rep. Gerry Studds of Massachusetts, who confessed to a homosexual affair with a male page in 1973, turned his back and faced House Speaker Thomas P. (Tip) O'Neill. . . .

The harsher sentences are in part a reaction to Studds' seemingly unrepentant insistence that his homosexual affair was a "voluntary, private relationship between adults." Disturbed that the pages were minors entrusted to congressional care, a few members even suggested that Studds . . . resign. ("The Hill Sex Scandal: Shame and Defiance," *Newsweek*, August 1, 1983, p. 28)

15–6 The same head of hair is never the same head of hair. (Label on a bottle of Finesse hair conditioner, November 1983)

15–7 Either God is the creator of the whole man, the whole universe, and all of reality, or He is the creator of none of it. (*A Christian Manifesto*, by Francis H. Schaeffer, p. 68)

15–8 ARTHRITIS SUFFERERS:

Arthritis Strength BUFFERIN reduces the inflammation the leading non-aspirin pain reliever can't.

Arthritis Strength BUFFERIN contains aspirin. And aspirin is the pain reliever doctors prefer for reduction of the painful inflammation that often accompanies arthritis.

Take Arthritis Strength BUFFERIN. It reduces the inflammation Tylenol and Extra Strength Tylenol can't. (Ad for Bufferin, *McCall's*, May 1982, p. 7)

15–9   Chapter 9 from *De Interpretatione*

by Aristotle

(Photocopied with the author's permission)

(Heading on a handout distributed at the President's Address at the 1982 conference of the Alabama Philosophical Society, U.A.B., Birmingham, Alabama, November 6, 1982)

15–10 The most basic rule of stratigraphy is that sedimentary rock formations on the bottom are older than those on the top. . . . However, this common-sense rule often seems not to work . . . .

". . . fossils have furnished, through their record of the evolution of life on this planet, an amazingly effective key to the relative positioning of strata . . ."

For true believers in evolution, it may be logical to date rocks this way . . . Since, however, we do not observe evolution taking place today, one must ask how they can be so confident that evolution was true in the past. The answer is that the evolutionary history of life is revealed by the fossil record in the sedimentary rocks. . . .

That is, ancient rocks contain fossils of organisms in an early stage of evolution; younger rocks contain fossils representing a more advanced stage of evolution. We know, of course, which rocks are ancient because they are the ones on the bottom, with the younger ones on top. But, then, we have just noted there are many places where this order is reversed. We know that they are reversed because of the evolutionary stage of their respective fossils.

Now, if one senses a feeling of dizziness at this point, it is because we are going in circles. ("Those Remarkable Floating Rock Formations," by Henry M. Morris, *Impact*, May 1983, p. i)

15–11 The UAB Holiday Party, previously held for faculty and staff during the second week of December, will not be held this year, President S. Richardson Hill, Jr., announced this week.

The president said growth in size of the university staff and financial constraints on UAB resulted in a decision not to hold the annual event.

Hill said, "We have sponsored a holiday party, based in University Hospitals cafeteria, for several years to give UAB faculty and staff an opportunity to come together and observe the spirit of the season as a family. . . .

"We will continue to plan and support activities which make employment at UAB beneficial to the human spirit as well as to one's economic needs." ("Holiday Party Is Cancelled," *U.A.B. Reports*, November 18, 1983, p. 1)

*15–12 Denton received an apology yesterday for a remark made late last week by George Lewis Bailes, state Democratic Party Chairman.

Bailes said that he had never known of a flag officer "dumb" enough to allow himself to be captured by the enemy. Denton was captured by the North Vietnamese when his plane was shot down in 1965 and remained a prisoner of war for seven years and seven months.

"My remarks were addressed to flag officers and were extemporaneously delivered in a political context as a generalization. My sincere apologies are hereby conveyed to each and every Alabama patriot offended by my remarks."

Denton said that the apology was incomplete.

"He keeps ignoring the fact that I was not a flag officer when I was shot down." ("Hurrahs Close Out Campaigns," *Birmingham Post-Herald*, November 4, 1980, p. A-1)

15–13 40% MORE PROTEIN FROM A GOLDEN GRIDDLE PANCAKE BREAKFAST
If you want your kids to have a nutritious breakfast that's also delicious, give them a hearty Golden Griddle breakfast of hot pancakes with Golden Griddle Syrup, orange juice and milk. IT CONTAINS 40% MORE PROTEIN THAN A TYPICAL BREAKFAST OF ORANGE JUICE, COLD CEREAL AND MILK. (Ad for Golden Griddle Pancake Syrup, *Working Mother*, February 1982, p. 24)

15–14 The French revolution was accomplished before it happened. ("A History of the Past: 'Life Reeked with Joy,' " compiled by Anders Henriksson, *Wilson Quarterly*, Spring 1983, p. 170)

*15–15 Roughly speaking, two pounds raw headless, unpeeled shrimp, properly cooked, will yield one pound of cooked, peeled and deveined shrimp—enough protein for six people. (Pamphlet, "Shrimp," published by the Gulf & South Atlantic Fisheries Development Foundation, Inc.)

15–16 There are two red herrings that are usually drawn across the trail at this point of the discussion: "Were the trees created with rings?" and, "Did Adam have a navel?" First, the question about the tree rings depends partially on the purpose for which God originally intended tree rings. We have observed this phenomenon and have noticed a correlation between the number of rings and the age of the tree, but chronology may be a secondary function of the rings, as indicated by certain trees that grow several rings in one year, or none at all, depending on weather conditions. Another possibility here is that God could have accelerated natural processes, so that He did in seconds what would normally have taken years to accomplish. Whether the tree had rings or not, the fact should not be overlooked that they were indeed mature and bearing fruit before the day was over (Gen. 1: 11–12). ("Starlight and the Age of the Universe," by Richard Niessen, *Impact*, July 1983, pp. iii–iv)

15-17   She says of herself: "I don't drink—only an occasional glass of vodka. My life is not a series of affairs. If I go out to dinner with somebody, I'm having an affair. That's ridiculous. Sex in itself is nothing. Unless there is some emotional tie, I'd rather play tennis.

"And drugs. Everybody assumes because I was married to a rock star . . . I did try cocaine, it made me schizophrenic. Mick was not a drug addict. He is a very disciplined man, with a strong sense of survival. Drugs are not a question of morals. People I've known and admired, I've watched disintegrate. They used drugs to lose a sense of loneliness until their physical and mental faculties were destroyed." ("Who Is Bianca Now?" by Marguerite Michaels, *Parade*, May 30, 1982, p. 13)

15-18   *The myth of the medically deprived.* Perpetrators of this myth insist that millions of poor citizens are sick, handicapped and doomed to early death because our health-care system neglects them. The truth is that patients from families earning less than $5000 annually averaged 5.8 physician-contacts in 1977 (latest figures available), as contrasted with only 4.7 contacts for families with an annual income of $10,000 or more. The lower-income group also spent more and longer periods in the hospitals. In the below-$5000 group, the average hospitalization was 1541 days per 1000 persons. That figure dropped steadily as income rose, with the most affluent group (annual income $25,000 or more) averaging 678.8 days per 1000 persons. ("Big Government and Hospital Care: Prescription for Disaster," by Drs. Michael and Lois DeBakey, *Reader's Digest*, December 1980, pp. 194–196)

15-19   "Another thing," she continued. "Your college sons must learn that one does not get the best out of employees by threatening them with bodily harm."

Obtaining an audience with son No. 1, I snarled, "I'll kill you if you threaten one of those kids again!" (" 'Six Hundred Bucks! And Nothing to It!' " by John G. Hubbel, *Reader's Digest*, May 1982, p. 105)

15-20   Noziere was a self-confessed young murderess of the thirties whose case became notorious largely because, having killed her father, she then complained of incest. Since she was almost certainly not his daughter, this seems rather hard cheese. ("All in the Family Way," a review by Derek Malcolm of the film *Violette Noziere, Manchester Guardian Weekly*, February 25, 1979, p. 6)

*15-21   The use of such materials as bloodroot, horehound and ylang ylang oil has declined in recent years, along with many other of the 500 or so natural ingredients used in foods, pharmaceuticals and cosmetics. Perhaps one reason, the book tells us, is that modern chemists, pharmacologists and food flavorists continue to place increasing emphasis on synthetically produced additives. (Review by Gordon Wilkinson of *Encyclopedia of Common Natural Ingredients Used in Foods, Drugs, and Cosmetics*, by A. Y. Leung, *New Scientist*, December 11, 1980, p. 724)

15-22 A subcommittee of the state Democratic Executive Committee said yesterday it made a mistake in disqualifying Lucile White in the Senate District 17 primary . . .

When asked if she felt her disqualification had anything to do with her participation in the National Organization for Women, she said, "The district is so conservative that there could have been questions about whether a candidate who professes liberal beliefs—which apparently meant being in favor of women, much less a person who was female herself—could be a viable candidate. I would think those people who subscribe to that kind of theory would have included being female a part of being a weak candidate." ("Ballot Error Revealed a Week Too Late," *Birmingham Post-Herald*, November 10, 1982, p. 1)

15-23 And the Lord God commanded man, saying, "You may freely eat of every tree of the garden; but the tree of the knowledge of good and evil you shall not eat, for in the day that you eat of it you shall die." (Gen. 2: 16–17)

15-24 Anacin-3 is 100% aspirin-free with the aspirin-free pain reliever doctors recommend most, pharmacists recommend most and hospitals use most.

In fact, you can't buy a safer, more effective aspirin-free pain reliever than Anacin-3. (Ad for Anacin-3, *Good Housekeeping*, September 1983, p. 3)

15-25 *What do you think college offers students today?* Somewhere between the ages of 14 and 22, there had better be contact with great ideas and the organizing of one's reaction to them. I meet a lot of young people of real potential—certainly all the potential I had— and they have not gone through the fire and therefore they're untempered. I often think how wonderful it would have been if they had some young Jesuit in philosophy or history knock them around. I think we have to put forth our ideas and have them jumped on by our elders and peers, stick with the things that are good, and discard the rubbish. I see no other way to educate oneself than by the interchange of ideas. ("Ask an Author: Q and A: James A. Michener," *Nutshell*, Fall 1981, p. 16)

15-26 7-DAY DEODORANT/ANTIPERSPIRANT

We know that the following example does not pertain to you, but when this great discovery was laboratory tested on people who were asked not to bathe for 7 days, they remained dry and odor-free the whole time! Imagine how effective 7-day Deodorant/ Antiperspirant will be for you with daily use. (*Hanover House Catalogue*, Fall 1983)

15-27 If you doubt that the American legal system serves the rich, consider the case of the paper bag versus the leather pouch. The U.S. Court of Appeals has held that paper bags may be searched without a warrant, but that your belongings are immune from warrantless search if you keep them in a zippered leather pouch. So be sure to get a Gucci for your gun . . . ("Tilting at Windmills," by Charles Peters, *Washington Monthly*, November 1980, p. 6)

15-28 The current level of federal expenditure on research and development is 8.4 billion dollars, which is around 10 percent of the federal budget, and 1.6 per cent of the gross national product. . . . The rate of increase of this budget item over the past 10 years has been 10 per cent per annum, which represents a doubling time of seven years. Since the doubling time of the GNP is around twenty years, at these present rates our government will be spending all of our money on science and technology in about sixty-five years. ("The Ethical Dimension of Scientific Research," by Nicholas Rescher, in *Beyond the Edge of Certainty*, ed. R. G. Colodny, p. 263)

15-29 As a Diesel, the 240D is designed to outflank many of those nickel-and-dime repairs and adjustments that can bedevil a gasoline engine and drive its maintenance costs up. (Ad for Mercedes-Benz, *Life*, June 1979, p. 40)

15-30 We are all acquainted with people who think they know a lot more than in fact they do. I'm thinking of fanatics, bigots, mystics, various types of dogmatists. And we have all heard of people who claim at least to know a lot less than what in fact they do know. I'm thinking of those people who call themselves "sceptics" . . .

　　If you have a healthy common sense, you will feel that there is something wrong with both of these extremes and that the truth is somewhere in the middle: we can know far more than the sceptic says we can know and far less than the dogmatist or the mystic says that he can know. (*The Problem of the Criterion*, by Roderick M. Chisholm, pp. 4–5)

15-31 Dear Abby: "Nora" asked, "Why would a man get upset because his wife or girlfriend wanted to see a male stripper?"

　　You replied: "Probably for the same reason some women get upset because their husbands or boyfriends want to see female strippers." (*Birmingham News*, April 20, 1982, p. 6B)

15-32 New studies reveal surprising help for high blood pressure.

　　Mazola.

　　New government and university studies showed proper diet can actually help reduce high blood pressure. Mazola Corn Oil was important in that diet. (Ad for Mazola, *Redbook*, December 1983, p. 12)

15-33 Touching this pylon means instant death. Anyone doing so will be subject to prosecution. (Notice on electricity pylon in Sussex, England)

15-34 Of course, concrete words as well as abstract ones get caught in this vortex of confusion. My favorite example is one I discovered while looking through a French dictionary many years ago. It defined *clocher* ("to limp") as *marcher en boitant* (roughly "to walk while hobbling") and *boiter* ("to hobble") as *clocher en marchant* ("to limp while walking"). This eager learner of French was helped precious little by that pair of definitions. ("Metamagical Themas," by Douglas R. Hofstadter, *Scientific American*, April 1983, p. 21)

15-35 Finding the right mortgage loan can be as difficult as finding the right home. Both have to be just right for how you live today. And how you plan to live tomorrow. That's why you should talk to the mortgage professional—SouthTrust Bank and its mortgage banking affiliate, Jackson Company. (Ad for SouthTrust Bank and Jackson Company, *Birmingham News*, November 23, 1983, p. 23B)

15-36 Dear Abby: My husband is in the paint business. A young widow in the next town asked him to paint her kitchen. He started four months ago and isn't finished yet. Abby, is this possible?

Dear Marion: How big is the lady's kitchen? ("Play it again, Abby," by Abigail Van Buren, *Reader's Digest*, October 1981, p. 122)

15-37 Richard Llewellyn, who died last week aged 26, was the most successful and widely read Welsh novelist of his time. Despite the fact that he was an exceedingly prolific writer who produced a wide range of novels over a 40-year period his success and his enduring fame were based on his first book. ("Hearts and Mines," by David Smith, *Manchester Guardian Weekly*, December 11, 1983, p. 6)

15-38 Thornton:
You are second in size to A.T.&T.?

McGowan:
Yes, we are.

Thornton:
Do you want to *be* A.T.&T.?

McGowan:
Ha, ha, ha. Well, this industry is so large, this is so unlike so many industries which have become deregulated, in that we are in a growth industry and everybody's got to build in order to satisfy the people's needs. And, so, I anticipate that they are going to do very well in it and we are going to do very well.

(William McGowan, president and chief operating officer of MCI, interviewed by Lee Thornton, "All Things Considered," NPR, WBHM, January 8, 1984)

15-39 In order to establish a more stable figure for velocity—the key number which ensures a stable link between money and prices—Friedman arbitrarily reduces the money stock by some 20 percent for a period of no less than 34 years between 1921 and 1955—nearly a third of the entire span he studies. This is on the grounds that "war and depression" cause people to hold more money in their bedsocks.

He also then boosts the price level in the period after the second world war to allow for price controls and rationing. In other words, Friedman argues that the price level must have been higher than official statistics showed, since the money supply grew more quickly than prices. He then uses the manipulated data to prove the link between money and prices. This is very circular, and very naughty. ("Why Milton's Monetarism Is Bunk," by Christopher Huhne, *Manchester Guardian Weekly*, December 25, 1983, p. 9)

15-40 "Well, Jesus," Rhoda said, beginning her prayer. "You know I have to get that ring back. So if you will get it back to me I promise I'll start believing in you." She waited a minute to let that sink in. ("Perils of the Nile," *In the Land of Dreamy Dreams*, by Ellen Gilchrist, p. 134)

15-41 There are some businessmen who think they can find sanctuary in the tall buildings of Makati. Let me tell you—we have pictures of everything that has happened where the faces of men are very clear. I repeat, even if it takes one whole year, you can rest assured we will look for you, not perhaps today because we are busy today attending to other serious problems, but there will be men assigned to track you down, legally applied by the government. I do not intend to threaten and intimidate, but I am telling you: do not test the force and strength of the government. (President Ferdinand Marcos of the Philippines talking about businessmen involved in street demonstrations against him, "All Things Considered," NPR, WBHM, Birmingham, Alabama, December 28, 1983)

15-42 I do it because I do it, because that's what I do. (Werner Erhard, the originator of est, quoted in "Powers of Mind," *Science: Good, Bad and Bogus*, by Martin Gardner, p. 304)

15-43 *On whether he should withdraw his nomination:* "I never considered it. I considered all the options but I decided against withdrawing, particularly after I discussed this with the president." (Edwin Meese, quoted in "Meese Speaks for Himself," *Newsweek*, April 2, 1984, p. 27)

15-44 Reagan himself shrugged off questions about [the propriety of some financial deals of] Meese last week by observing that Meese, like many of his appointees, had made "some pretty great economic sacrifices . . . to work for the government." ("County-Club Ethics?" by Tom Morganthau, *Newsweek*, April 2, 1984, p. 28)

Section 16

Fallacies Four

Unknowable Statistics
Faulty Comparison
Insignificant Changes
Questionable Baseline or Period
Gambler's Fallacy
Small Sample
Unrepresentative Sample
Bad Polling Techniques

Introduction

The topic of the examples in this final section is bad argumentation connected with the use of numbers and statistics.

Of course, any of the fallacies covered in the previous three sections can also involve statistics. However, although there is an enormous potential for incorrect argumentation connected with statistics (a potential that is often deliberately exploited), there are relatively few named statistical fallacies.

Two genuine statistical fallacies are as follows:

Fallacy of Unknowable Statistics

This argument gives questionable numerical estimates of phenomena. It usually takes the form of giving too precise a figure, for example, when someone "guesstimates" some value to be, say, 8,464 when there is absolutely no way in which such an estimate could be accurate to more than the nearest one hundred. In such a situation, the "guesstimate" should be rounded out to the nearest one hundred. This fallacy also occurs when, for example, an average is calculated to a degree of accuracy beyond the accuracy of the raw figures on which it is based—for instance, when the average salary of some group is calculated to the last cent from the raw data of the individuals' off-the-cuff responses to a pollster.

Fallacy of Faulty Comparison

This fallacy consists in making a comparison of some feature of two different things where, because of other differences, the comparison is rendered useless and misleading. (Faulty comparison might be considered to be a statistical version of the fallacy of questionable classification.)

There are two further fallacies having to do with statistics:

Fallacy of Insignificant Changes

The insignificant changes fallacy argues that some change in a phenomenon has occurred, where there indeed is a change in the statistics but where the change is so small compared with the absolute values that it might be owing to nothing more than chance fluctuation. An example of this fallacy is arguing that an apple tree is less productive this year because, whereas it produced 444 apples last year, it produced only 440 this year.

Fallacy of Questionable Baseline (or Period)

In this fallacy the argument makes claims about percentage changes without making clear what is the baseline on which the percentage change is calculated and/or not making clear the period over which the change occurs.

Another fallacy is usually considered along with statistical fallacies:

Gambler's Fallacy

Here a person argues that because something has happened in the past, it is less likely to occur in the future, where, in fact, the future occurrences (or nonoccurrences) are totally independent of past occurrences. For example, arguing that because your house has been hit by meteorites on the two previous nights it is a lot less likely to get hit again tonight than are previously unhit houses is a gambler's fallacy.

Some statistical fallacies have to do with sampling and drawing conclusions about the class of things from which the sample came (that is, the population):

Fallacy of Small Sample

This argument makes a conclusion about the population, where the size of the sample is too small in comparison with the size of the population for such a conclusion to be drawn.

Fallacy of Unrepresentative Sample

This argument makes a conclusion about the occurrence of some feature in a population, where the sample used as evidence is biased with respect to that feature—that is, the rate of occurrence of that feature in the sample is different from the rate of occurrence in the total population.

Fallacy of Bad Polling Techniques

This is conducting the polling of a sample in such a way that the results are likely not to be representative of the whole population. There is a range of ways in which polling techniques can be bad. Questions can be badly (or skillfully, depending on your point of view) worded to result in incorrect conclusions. Questioning people might not get at the true facts because people tend to be less ready to report (or even remember) less flattering things about themselves than more flattering things. Moreover, people are likely not to be honest in response to questions about illegal or socially frowned upon habits: Polling adults in a shopping center about their use of marijuana isn't likely to get very accurate results; polling adults about their consumption of alcohol is likely to yield more accurate results than a similar poll among schoolchildren.

More comprehensive discussions of statistical fallacies are given in these texts:

Howard Kahane, *Logic & Contemporary Rhetoric*, 4th ed., Ch. 5
Stephen K. Campbell, *Flaws and Fallacies in Statistical Thinking*

Follow the instructions in Section 13 for the discussion of fallacies in general. Be careful to examine the exercises for statistical problems other than those covered by the fallacies named in this section.

Section 16: Exercises

16–1 The British Isles by some estimates had 201 famines between 10 A.D. and 1846. (*The Big, Fertile, Rumbling, Cast-Iron, Growling, Aching, Unbuttoned Bellybook*, by James Trager, p. 4)

16–2 HAPPINESS LOVES COMPANY

In an age when many car owners are less than ecstatic, statistics show that 9 out of 10 new Volvo owners are happy.

In the case of this particular group from Washington, D.C., the statistic is 10 out of 10.

These people are so happy with their Volvos they've formed a club. They have picnics, car rallies and regular monthly meetings. They swap Volvo stories and tell Chevy jokes. They compare notes on how dependable their Volvos are. (Some of these cars have gone hundreds of thousands of miles.) They even put out a club newsletter and pay dues.

All because they love the cars they own.

If you've never felt this kind of affection for a car you've owned, buy a Volvo.

You may never join a Volvo fan club. But the odds are you'll become a Volvo fan.

VOLVO—A car you can believe in. (Ad for Volvo, *People*, April 9, 1979, pp. 98–99. Reprinted by permission)

16–3 UAB ENROLLMENT RISES DESPITE NATIONAL TREND

Enrollment for the Fall '82–'83 quarter was 14,530, up from 14,474 the previous year. (*Kaleidoscope*, February 15, 1983, p. 1)

16–4 My wife and I have been happily married for years. Up to this time, our relationship has been monogamous, but we've been talking about extramarital affairs recently. She said that she did not object to them in principle but that she had read somewhere that fooling around was bad for your health. She is not referring to crimes of passion or jealous lovers but, rather, to the chance of having a heart attack while making love to a mistress. It sounds like an old wives' tale to me. Is there any truth to the story?—J. R., New York, N.Y.

Uh, we hate to be the bearer of bad news, but your wife is on to something. The chances of having a heart attack while making love are infinitesimal, but if you do have one, the chances are that you will have it with your mistress and not with your wife. A study of 34 cardiac patients who died during intercourse revealed that 29 of the 34 were having an extramarital affair. We don't know what this means; we're not sure we want to. (*Playboy*, December 1978, p. 67. Copyright © 1978 by Playboy. Reprinted by permission)

16-5 In the past 6 years I've had 3 TVs, 6 picture tubes, and one 'fridge—a Frigidaire. (TV ad for Frigidaire, Fall 1981)

16-6 It [the 1981 Census of the Republic of India] turned up the numbing total of 683,810,051. Ask not how they came to reach a figure of such finesse as to include that final convincing One, when as everyone knows the Indian nation's population increases by several thousand every *minute*, and the enumerators well know that by the time they had totted up the total it was already wildly short of reality. ("Since Independence, the Population Has Doubled," by James Cameron, *Manchester Guardian Weekly*, April 26, 1981, p. 9)

16-7 Horror movies enjoy a massive following among teen-agers, but younger children are finding them too scary and violent, making them regret ever having seen them.

   A new study by psychologist Joanne Cantor of the University of Wisconsin and Sandra Reilly, Development Director of Edgewood High School in Madison, Wis., reveals that horror movies may be too frightening for some kids, and more violent than their parents think they are.

   In a survey of 81 children aged between 12 and 16, the researchers found that scary movies left a lasting and harmful impression on most children.

   Fully 55 percent said that a scary movie made them feel nervous and gave them nightmares and trouble getting to sleep.

   As a result, 30 percent of the children said they deliberately avoided watching some other horror movie because they thought it might be too scary.

   Scary movies were so upsetting to 32 percent of the students that they said they regretted ever watching some movies and wished they could forget the whole experience.

   Nevertheless, horror movies still remain enormously popular among teens, with 80 percent saying they enjoy them frequently.

   At least 55 percent said they recently watched a horror movie in a theater and 76 percent recently saw one on television. ("Scary Movies Giving Kids Nightmares," *Star*, November 9, 1982. Reprinted by permission.)

*16-8 Since the first hospital opened in Shreveport, Louisiana, in 1922, there have been approximately 349,492 operations performed. There have been 304,245 braces and prostheses applied, approximately 3,642,364 x-rays and photos taken, 6,351,624 physical therapy treatments given and 2,624,217 clinic visits. ("1982 Shriners Hospitals Facts and Figures," *Zamora Temple Shrine Hospital News*, October 1983, p. 3)

*16-9 In a nine year study of 51 battered infants, two doctors of the Montreal Children's Hospital in Canada found that 12 of the infants, or 23.5%, were infants weighing below normal at birth.

   Since only 7 to 8 percent of infants born in Quebec are low in weight, the two doctors concluded in July *American Journal of Disease of Children* that low birth weight may well contribute to child-beating. (*National Enquirer*, October 24, 1982, p. 29)

16–10   54% of the men tested found Bic shavers equal to or better than Trac II. (Ad for Bic Shavers, WBRC-TV, Birmingham, Alabama, November 22, 1980)

16–11   CANADIANS FINE AD AGENCY FOR ZENITH TV COMMERICAL

The commercial for Zenith color TV said . . . that the repairers named Zenith sets easiest to fix and preferred to own Zenith over any other brand. When the commercial ran in Canada, it was backed by a survey of 501 Canadian TV repairers.

The ad agency, Foote, Cone & Belding Advertising Ltd., found itself brought before a criminal court when the prosecutor for the Crown had the survey examined by standard statistical methods and found surprising discrepancies. . . .

The statements in the commercial were technically true, based on some of the raw data. But the ad agency had made no adjustment to account for the fact that not all the service-people were equally familiar with every brand. When the data were weighed in proportion to the repairers' knowledge about each brand, very different results emerged; although Zenith was highly regarded by the repairers, it did not emerge statistically higher than Motorola, Philips, Electohome, Hitachi, or Panasonic. (Copyright 1980 by Consumers Union of United States, Inc., Mount Vernon, N.Y. 10553. Reprinted by permission from *Consumer Reports*, February 1980)

*16–12   "Why is it that Alabama, a State with 10% of the Nation's natural resources, can rank so low in so many important areas?"

- 47th out of the 50 states in support for law enforcement
- 44th out of the 50 states in funding for education
- 12th out of the 14 Southern states in personal income growth from 1970–1980
- 13th out of the 14 Southern states in economic growth in urban areas
- LAST out of the 14 Southern states in attracting new jobs and industries

"I'm tired of Alabama being last." (*Annual Report to the People of Alabama*, from Lt. Gov. George McMillan, 1982, p. 2)

16–13   Detroit (AP)—The five major domestic automakers reported a sales decline of 9.9 percent in the first 10 days of January for the lowest daily selling rate since the same period in 1975. . . .

Only Chrysler Corp. had a sales increase, up 4 percent. Volkswagen of America's 52.1 percent decline was the biggest drop. General Motors Corp. was off 7.4 percent and Ford Motor Company was down 21.9 percent. American Motors Corp., which does not give 10-day figures, was estimated to have a slide of 18.3 percent. ("Automakers Report More Sales Drops," *Birmingham News*, January 14, 1982, p. 4D)

16–14   U.S. CUTTING TROOPS ON TAIWAN

Hong Kong—In a sign of its continued interest in normalization of relations with Peking, the Carter administration has reduced the number of U.S. military personnel on Taiwan to 750, about half the size of the U.S. force there a year ago. . . .

At the current rate of withdrawal, the number would decline to about 600 by the end of this year and all military personnel would be gone by the end of next year. (*Washington Post* section, *Manchester Guardian Weekly*, November 12, 1978)

16-15   The number of state employees had been increasing at a rate of 16 percent until 1979. Since then, the number of state employees has been reduced 1.44 percent. (*A Special Report to the People of Alabama*, from Governor Fob James, 1982, p. 6)

16-16   DRIVE UP YOUR NET WORTH IN A RABBIT

$4220,* new '78; $4350,† resale '79; $4400,† resale '80

*Manufacturer's suggested '78 retail price—Rabbit 2-door hatchback. P.O.E., Local taxes and other dealer delivery charges extra.
†Resale prices as quoted in NADA Official Used Car Guide, January '79, '80 Eastern Editions are average retail prices, not trade-in and do not include local taxes. (Ad for Volkswagen, *Newsweek*, June 9, 1980, p. 108)

16-17   Boston (AP)—Nobel Laureate Linus Pauling says there's evidence that Laetrile and metabolic therapy have some value against cancer, despite a major study that found the combination to be worthless.

In a letter in today's *New England Journal of Medicine*, Pauling criticized the conclusions of a Mayo Clinic study conducted for the National Cancer Institute.

"It's my opinion," he wrote, "that there probably was a beneficial effect, including prolongation of survival." (Pauling, who won the Nobel Prize for chemistry in 1954, noted that cancer patients treated with Laetrile and metabolic therapy survived an average of almost five months. He said other studies have shown that people with incurable cancer ordinarily survive about 1-1/2 months.) ("Nobel Winner Disagrees with Laetrile Study," *Birmingham News*, July 8, 1982, p. 8A)

16-18   You don't have to be neurotic to be rich, but it helps. . . . Lee Benham, an economist, and Alexandra Benham, a mathematician, made the finding after analyzing information about 283 white men, all of whom had been interviewed as children in the 1920s and again 30 years later.

Ninety-four of the men were classified as mentally well; the rest had some form of mental illness.

Forty-four of them were diagnosed as neurotics, a term no longer used by mental health professionals, but which was defined in the 1950s as a disorder characterized by anxiety . . .

The Benhams found that the neurotics earned 23 percent more than those considered well . . .

They are unable, however, to answer the chicken-or-egg question: Does being neurotic lead to a higher income? Or does a higher income lead to neurosis? ("Money and

Neuroses: Chicken Then Egg?" by David Wessel, *Birmingham News*, July 8, 1982, p. 4D. Reprinted by permission)

*16–19 The 6:00 A.M. news on November 4, 1980, WBHM, Birmingham, Alabama, stated that early results indicated Reagan would win the election. The evidence was the results from Dixville, New Hampshire, where the polls had closed after all 24 registered voters had cast their votes: 17 had voted for Reagan, whereas only 3 had voted for Carter. The newscaster further stated that this community had "predicted" the results of elections twice in the last 20 years.

16–20 Brenner severely criticized Percival Lowell's estimate of the rotation period of Venus. Brenner himself compared two drawings of Venus in white light made by two different people four years apart—from which he deduced a rotation period of 23 hours, 57 minutes and 36.37728 seconds, which he said agreed well with the mean of his own "most reliable" drawings. ("The Past and Future of American Astronomy," *Broca's Brain: Reflections on the Romance of Science*, by Carl Sagan, p. 261)

16–21 Zoback and his colleagues say the odds are 100% that Parkfield [California] will soon have a "quake quite definitely big enough to feel." Indeed, USGA researchers predict the "quake will hit in January of 1988, give or take four years." ("All Things Considered," NPR, WBHM, January 23, 1984)

16–22 That night [the night of the first U.S. appearance of The Beatles, on the Ed Sullivan Show] Ed Sullivan had the largest television audience ever to watch an entertainment program. It's been said that, during the show, America's crime rate was lower than it had been in 50 years. Police stations in New York City documented a sudden drop in juvenile delinquency—they say that not a single hubcap was stolen. ("All Things Considered," NPR, WBHM, February 6, 1984)

16–23 Despite . . . limitations on the traditional approaches to caries prevention, most people accord them high priority. In a recent issue of *Dental Hygiene*, Alice M. Horowitz, coordinator of health-education activities for the National Institute of Dental Research, summarized a typical survey of public perceptions about tooth decay. In the survey, which was conducted in 1980, 653 Minnesota adults were asked what they thought was the best way to avoid getting cavities. Sixty-one percent chose oral-hygiene measures; 15 percent said visiting the dentist; and 12 percent advised avoiding sweets.

Only about 1 percent mentioned the use of fluoride (beyond its use in toothpastes). ("Tooth Decay: The Early Problem," *Consumer Reports*, March 1984, p. 130)

16–24 There are more people at work in the United States today than at any time in the history of the United States of America. (Vice-President George Bush, "All Things Considered," NPR, WBHM, March 10, 1984)

WORKED EXERCISES

Section 1

1–2 No use/mention quotes are needed in this passage. The quotes around 'reason' are scare quotes indicating that the word is being used in an unusual way. Strictly speaking, only sentient beings can reason; as computers are (at least, so far) not sentient, to say that they reason is to use 'reason' in an extended way.

1–6 Use/mention quotes need to be added around 'détente':

> You know, and I know, that 'détente' is a word that will last only as long as the balance of power exists.

1–9 The double quotes round the whole passage are direct quotes indicating that these are the exact words Senator Byrd used. The single quotes around 'd' are use/mention quotes indicating that the letter 'd' is being mentioned. There should also be use/mention quotes around the second occurrence of 'democratic':

> "In my opinion the delegates should not be bound to vote for any particular candidate . . . This would be the democratic way—and I am spelling 'democratic' with a small 'd'. "

1–33 Use/mention quotes are needed around 'hammock' and 'hurricane'. The passage attempts to use *and* mention the word 'tobacco' at the same time. To put this more satisfactorily, the beginning of the second sentence is rewritten slightly:

> Then it [Havana] became the main port and assembly point for the trans-shipment to Spain of the vast treasures extracted from the Western hemisphere. Coffee, tobacco (like 'hammock' and 'hurricane', 'tobacco' is an original Carib word), and later sugar added to the burgeoning wealth of the great city.

Section 2

2–3 This passage gives a *partial* definition of 'pronation' and 'supination'. It gives the same definition for both terms, but, presumably, 'pronation' and 'supination' have different meanings; so there must be two different kinds of side-to-side motion of the foot. Adequate definitions would specify what type of side-to-side motion each of the terms refers to.

2-5 This is a stipulative definition—giving an account of the extended way in which 'married' is to be used in a special area of discourse (State Farm Insurance documents).

2-6 This is an unsuccessful attempt to give a partial definition of 'genuine literature'. Jane Austen wrote genuine literature, but she could hardly be considered a social outcast, political exile, misfit, or heretic. She, and many other authors who are counterexamples to this "definition," show that it is not satisfactory.

2-14 This is a statement of the fact that it is difficult to give any very precise definition of 'soul food'. An example of something (collards) that definitely qualifies as soul food is given; and then an amusing definition (that is not intended to be technically satisfactory) is offered.

Section 3

3-10 'MAYDAY' is the international distress signal. It is homophonous with the French expression 'M'Aidez', which means *help me*—which gives the etymology of the term.

3-16 This item involves both ambiguity and homophony. 'Bucks' can refer to male deer or can be used as slang for 'dollars'—and is thus ambiguous. 'Doe', which refers to a female deer, is a homophone with 'dough', a slang term for money. The "joke" is based on ambiguity and homophony as what is referred to by this ambiguous term and the homophones are either animals or money.

3-30 This item is ambiguous because various expressions in it are ambiguous. 'Hot' can either mean *high in temperature* or *spicy and peppery*; the ad could be claiming that their food is served lukewarm or that it is not too spicy. 'Not so hot' can also mean *not very good*; they could be advertising that they have mediocre food. Finally, 'hot' can also mean *stolen*—so the ad could be construed as saying that they serve less stolen food (than their competitors?). (It might not surprise you to know that Pedro's is no longer in business.)

3-34 The first sentence of the passage refers to a person and a programming language, both having the name 'Ada'. When the second sentence states that a more extended history of the early development of Ada is given in some book, it is unclear whether the book gives the person's history or the history of the language. (*Presumably*, it is the language.) This is an example of referential ambiguity of a name—a name referring to two quite distinct things.

Section 4

4-1 *James Michener's U.S.A.* is <u>bubble-headed</u> from the first page to the last. By contrast, even Michener's <u>leaden, interminable</u> novels are works of art. This book aims to <u>exploit</u> his popularity and gives his readers <u>nothing of value</u> in return—unless you count 17 pictures of James A. Michener, which is the number found herewith. By turns he looks kindly, public spirited, grandfatherly and wise: by lending his name to this enterprise, he also looks <u>greedy</u>.

James Michener's U.S.A. is light and frothy from first page to last. It contrasts remarkably with his novels which are, in comparison, weighty, solid, extended works of art. This book is aimed at a reading population with which Michener is highly popular, and although it doesn't overload the reader with new facts and views, it has the bonus of 17 pictures of Michener himself. By turns he appears kindly, public spirited, grandfatherly and wise: by lending his name to this new enterprise, he also seems to have a good idea of what will be a successful publishing adventure.

4–5 British Airways has moved to <u>shore up</u> its <u>sagging</u> finances by <u>offloading</u> two of its new Boeing 757 jet aircraft almost two years before they are delivered from the manufacturers. In a highly complex deal, British Airways is to allow Air Europe, the charter and package tour arm of Intasun Leisure, to take over two of the 19 new 757s. The arrangement will <u>save</u> the <u>struggling</u> State-owned airline around £40 million and <u>ease the burden</u> of meeting the £400 million cost of the original 757 package.

The deal follows strenuous efforts by BA management to "reschedule" the 757 deal, by taking delivery of the new jets over four years instead of the planned three.

British Airways has moved to improve its financial situation which had previously not looked quite so promising. It has enterprisingly sold two of its new Boeing 757 jet aircraft two years before they are even delivered from the manufacturers. In a highly complex deal, British Airways is to allow Air Europe, the charter and package tour arm of Intasun Leisure, to take over two of the 19 new 757s. The arrangement will net the State-owned airline around £40 million, which will considerably improve its finances. This will pay one-tenth the cost of the original 757 package deal.

The deal follows strenuous efforts by BA management to "reschedule" the 757 deal, by taking delivery of the new jets over four years instead of the planned three.

4–9 The term 'action oriented' to describe the curriculum is clearly chosen because of its upbeat connotation. Terms such as 'work oriented', 'job oriented', 'occupation oriented', and 'employment oriented' are much more accurate descriptively but presumably were avoided because they do not have such positive connotations as 'action oriented'.

4–14 Margaret Thatcher, née Roberts, was a <u>dreadful</u> child who grew into a <u>dreadful</u> woman. So <u>prissy</u> was she that classmates would devise circuitous routes to school to <u>avoid</u> meeting her on the way. Fellow students at Oxford detected an <u>unattractive</u> tendency to <u>manipulate</u> people. At her first job, as a chemist in a plastics factory, she was nicknamed "Duchess" because she was so <u>haughty</u>. Denis liked her but his parents shared the general <u>unfavorable</u> view. Her only recorded hobby is interior decorating.

Margaret Thatcher, née Roberts, as a child inspired awe, and she continues to do so as an adult. She was a very proper child who, because of this, was avoided by children of different standards. Fellow students at Oxford noticed an ability to influence and guide people, which, of course, some of them did not value. In her original profession—a chemist in the plastics industry—she was named "Duchess" by some unkind workers because she appeared to be superior to them. Denis Thatcher liked her, and his parents' views were similar to those of others who knew her. Her busy professional life has left time for only one recorded hobby—that of interior design.

Section 5

5-3   <I can either run this hotel> *or* <look after Tallulah Bankhead>. I can't do *both*.

(I can run this hotel OR I can look after Tallulah Bankhead) AND NOT (I can run this hotel AND I can look after Tallulah Bankhead)

5-11   *Unless* <we dramatically improve funding for education>, *and* <in particular teacher salaries>, <our children> *and* <their children will not have the opportunity for the quality education that was ours>.

(We dramatically improve funding for education AND we dramatically improve funding for teacher salaries) OR (NOT Our children will have the opportunity for the quality education that was ours AND NOT Our children's children will have the opportunity for the quality education that was ours)

5-20   <A map in your ad> <will help people find you>.

IF You put a map in your ad THEN People will be helped in finding you

5-25   <Buster and Mr. Lewis been knowing each other for a long time>.

This is a simple sentence. We might think that it could be split into the two conjuncts 'Buster been knowing Mr. Lewis for a long time' and 'Mr. Lewis been knowing Buster for a long time'. However, the sense of 'know' involved here seems such that each of the "conjuncts" entails the other—which indicates that they really say the same thing. Thus they are not genuinely different statements, and the original passage is a simple sentence.

Section 6

6-3   < ① The 1850s and 1860s were boom decades [in Britain]>. < ② British exports grew more rapidly in the first seven years of the 1850s than in any other period of the nation's history>.

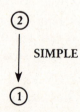

6-10 < ①L'Anse-aux-Meadows is probably Vinland>. <② It is, at any rate, the only authenticated site of a Norse Viking settlement in North America>.

< ② L'Anse-aux-Meadows is the only authenticated site of a Norse Viking settlement in North America>

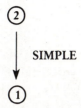

6-21 < ① The pop operation cannot be applied to the empty stack> (because) <② such a stack has no elements to delete>. (Therefore,) < ③ before applying the pop operation to a stack, we must ensure that the stack is not empty>.

< ② An empty stack has no elements to delete>

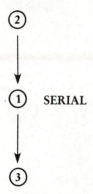

6-30 < ① The simplest things can present problems>. < ② André must use a pencil to dial a telephone>, (because) < ③ his fingers won't fit in the holes in the dial>.

< ③ André's fingers won't fit in the holes in the dial of a telephone>

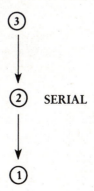

The final conclusion has been left broadly stated. We might argue that something more restricted is intended—perhaps 'The simplest things can present problems for a giant' or 'The simplest things can present problems for André'.

Section 7

7-2 < ① AMERICANS GETTING TOO SALTY >

< ② Only one gram of sodium a day is enough to sustain the human body in normal health >, say researchers at the University of Massachusetts in Amherst.

Unfortunately, they report, < ③ the average American consumes between five and 15 grams of sodium in table salt each day >.

< ① The average American is consuming too much salt >

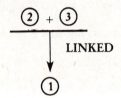

$$\frac{② + ③}{}$$

LINKED

①

7-10 (Two important points have been clearly identified by) < ① the Soviet attack on KAL Flight 007 >: (1.) < ② The Soviets do not recognize individual rights >; (2.) > ③ The Soviets cannot be trusted >.

< ① The Soviets attacked KAL Flight 007 >

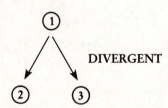

DIVERGENT

7-11 (There are two main reasons why) < ① someone might buy a six-month bank certificate instead of going for the higher yields of a money-market fund >.

(The first is that) < ② these certificates are insured by an agency of the Federal government >.

(The second is that) < ③ a certificate enables you to lock up your 9 percent, or whatever rate you are getting, for the next six months >.

< ① A person should buy a six-month bank certificate instead of going for the higher yields of a money-market fund >

< ② Six-month bank certificates are insured by an agency of the Federal government >
< ③ Six-month bank certificates enable a person to lock up the 9 percent, or whatever rate he is getting, for the next six months >

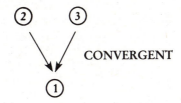

CONVERGENT

7-12   < ① The New Balance 990 is the most technologically sophisticated running shoe made today >.

< ② It has a unique polyurethane Motion Control Device for maximum stability >. < ③ A midsole unit made of three different layers of EVA for shock absorption >. And < ④ a *new* Superflex outersole with a carbon rubber heel pad for durability >.

< ① The New Balance 990 is the most technologically sophisticated running shoe made in September 1983 >

< ② The New Balance 990 has a unique polyurethane Motion Control Device for maximum stability >

< ③ The New Balance 990 has a midsole unit made of three different layers of EVA for shock absorption >

< ④ The New Balance 990 has a *new* Superflex outersole with a carbon rubber heel pad for durability >

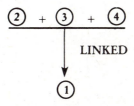

LINKED

We might think that the argument in this passage is convergent rather than linked. Each of the reasons is, alone, a reason for saying that the New Balance 900 is a technologically sophisticated shoe; however, as any one of these features alone might be something that another shoe has, it would seem that the fact that the New Balance 990 has all three features gives better support for the conclusion that this is *the most* technologically sophisticated shoe. (Whereas another shoe might have one of these features, it is less likely that any other shoe has all three.) Therefore, diagramed as linked, the argument is stronger than diagramed as convergent; and as the argument should be presented in the way most favorable to its author, it is best represented as linked.

Section 8

8-5   < ① The proper temperature in most instances is 365° >, < ② as easy to remember as the number of days in the year >.

< ① In most instances, the proper temperature for deep-fat frying is 365° >
< ② The proper temperature for most instances of deep-fat frying is as easy to remember as the number of days in the year >
< ③ The number of days in the year is 365 >

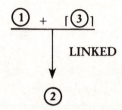

8-24   Thousands of iron supplement pills made from freeze-dried seal liver were ordered withdrawn from the market: < ① The pills, sold ironically in health food stores, contained up to 60 ppm of mercury >. Said the president of the firm which made the pills, "Seal liver attracted my attention because < ② it came from an animal most free of contaminants >. You can just figure from this that < ③ there isn't any place in the whole earth that isn't contaminated >.

< ① Thousands of iron supplement pills made from freeze-dried seal liver contained up to 60 ppm of mercury >
< ② The seal is the animal most free of contaminants >

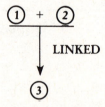

8-26   < ① BE SEEN > ...
< ② Advertise in the BELL SYSTEM YELLOW PAGES >

< ① You want to be seen >
< ② You should advertise in the Bell System Yellow Pages >
< ③ If you want to be seen then you should advertise in the Bell System Yellow Pages >

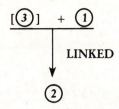

8-29 The frequent claim that no < ① true scientist can be a Bible-believing Christian or creationist > is refuted by the fact that < ② the greatest scientists of earlier generations did believe in the Bible and in God as Creator >.

< ① A true scientist can be a Bible-believing Christian or creationist >

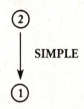

Section 9

9-11 < ① Contrary to the public image of dinosaurs as the Edsels of evolution >, says Colbert, < ② they were extraordinarily well-adapted creatures >. < ③ They inhabited every corner of the world > and < ④ ranged in bulk from the chicken-sized < ⑤ Compsognathus > to the < ⑥ 100-ton Brachiosaurus >, the largest creature ever to tread the earth >. Though they plodded through swamps and shallow coastal waters, they were essentially land bound. < ⑦ Some ambled on all fours >; < ⑧ others scampered after prey on their lower limbs >. < ⑨ Some may have lived a century or more >.

< ① Dinosaurs were not the Edsels of evolution >
< ② Dinosaurs were extraordinarily well-adapted creatures >
< ③ Dinosaurs inhabited every corner of the world >
< ④ Dinosaurs ranged in bulk from chicken-sized to the largest creature ever to tread the earth >
< ⑤ Compsognathus, a dinosaur, was the size of a chicken >
< ⑥ Brachisosaurus, a dinosaur, weighed 100 tons >
< ⑦ Some dinosaurs ambled on all fours >
< ⑧ Some dinosaurs scampered after prey on their lower limbs >
< ⑨ Some dinosaurs may have lived a century or more >

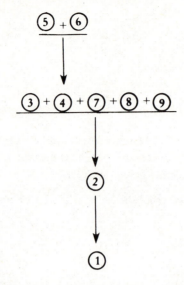

9-13 < ① Unwrap your fragrant soap and place it in dresser drawers > < ② to impart its aroma to your belongings >. < ③ The soap will harden, unwrapped >, and < ④ last much longer when you do start to use it >.

< ② Unwrapped fragrant soap in your dresser drawers will impart its aroma to your belongings >
< ③ Unwrapped soap in your dresser drawers will harden >
< ④ Hardened soap will last much longer when it is used >

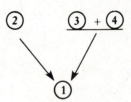

9-25 "< ① There are a lot of 'dryer only' purchases > (because) < ② a dryer usually lasts longer than a washer >," said Joy Schrage, manager of communications for the Whirlpool Corp. in Benton Harbor, Mich.

"< ③ An automatic washer lasts an average of 11 years >. < ④ A gas dryer lasts about 13 years >. And < ⑤ an electric dryer lasts about 15 years >."

< ⑥ A dryer lasts from 13 to 15 years >

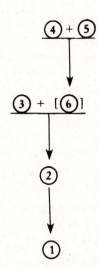

9–35 < ① The computer increasingly lets knowledge be something that can immediately be used, rather than something that must be simply learned for an exam >. (Another) < ② important benefit of using the computer as a tool for discovery > is that < ③ most students find it fun to play with computers, trying out their ideas for new programs > and (so) < ④ students can get enjoyably involved in their work >.

< ② There are important benefits to using the computer as a tool for discovery > < ④ With computers, students can get enjoyably involved in their work >

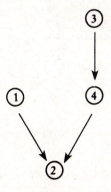

Section 10

10–2 "By < ① taking off and landing at night >, (you've proven that) < ② the [space] shuttle [Challenger] is capable of operating under most any conditions >," President Reagan told the crew.

< ① The space shuttle Challenger took off and landed at night >

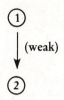

(weak)

10-3 < ① Now, did Adam have a navel? Probably not >, (simply because) < ② the navel
is a remnant of the normal birth process, and not of maturity or functionality >.
(Therefore,) < ③ for God to have created him with one would indeed be deception >, (because) < ④ it would convey misleading information >.

< ① Adam probably did not have a navel >
< ③ For God to have created Adam with a navel would indeed be deception >
< ④ Adam having a navel would convey misleading information >
< ⑤ God would not create misleading information >

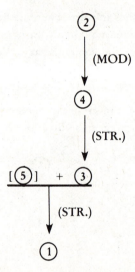

10-9 < ① Sartre has been called the conscience of his generation. Unquestionably < ② he
was too often wrong > for that >.

< ① Sartre was not the conscience of his generation >
< ② Sartre was very often wrong >

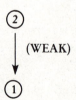

10–11 Gastronomic writers repeat endlessly that < ① Cicero was so called because he had a wart on his nose the size of a chicken-pea (cicer, in Latin); but this can hardly be so> ... (for)< ② Cicero was not his nickname, it was his family name>, < ③ which antedated his wart by countless generations>.

< ① Cicero was not called 'Cicero' because of the wart the size of a chick-pea on his nose>
< ② 'Cicero' was not Cicero's nickname, but his family name>
< ③ Cicero's family name antedated Cicero's wart by countless generations>

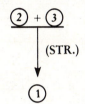

Section 11

11–3 Either < ① this is the best space game ever>, or < ② my living room is going 165 m.p.h.>

< ① Intellivision Star Strike is the best space game ever>

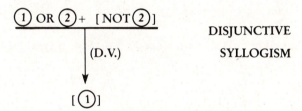

DISJUNCTIVE

SYLLOGISM

11–7 The argument in this passage is completely in the question:

< ① Zsa Zsa Gabor, who recently got married for the eighth time, gave her age as 54>. If <① that's true> < ② she was only 5 when she entered and won the Miss Hungary beauty title in 1933>. How old is Zsa Zsa really?

< ① Zsa Zsa Gabor is 54>
< ② Zsa Zsa Gabor was only 5 when she entered and won the Miss Hungary beauty title in 1933>

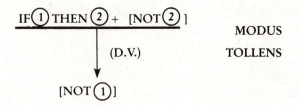

MODUS

TOLLENS

11–16 < ① You are either good > <u>or</u> < ② bad >, and both < ③ are dangerous >. < ④ Go
away >.

< ① You are good >
< ② You are bad >
< ③ You are dangerous >
< ④ You should go away >

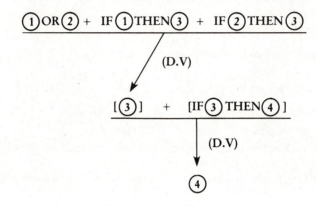

11–25 This passage is too chaotic to be usefully marked up. Instead, the deductive argument
that is contained in it is presented in a diagram that uses complete sentences instead of
numbers for sentences:

IF A. A. Milne feared bears THEN A. A. Milne would have written as if he loved Winnie-
the-Pooh

+

A. A. Milne wrote as if he loved Winnie-the-Pooh

(INVAL.)

AFFIRMING THE
CONSEQUENT

A. A. Milne feared bears

Section 12

12–2 < ① Add naught to MacNaughton > — (because) < ② you don't dilute a great
Canadian Whisky >.

< ① All MacNaughton whisky should have nothing added to it >
< ② All great Canadian whiskies should have nothing added to them >
[< ③ All MacNaughton whisky is great Canadian whisky >]

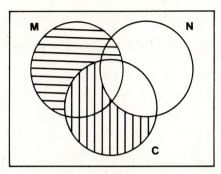

KEY
M abbreviates the class of
   MacNaughton whiskies
N abbreviates the class of things that
   should have nothing added to them
C abbreviates the class of great
   Canadian whiskies

12-6   < ① Madelyn, ~~a Cherokee Indian, came to ICO 12 years ago when~~ the Boy Scouts of
America told her she could not be the leader of her son's scouting troop > (because),
< ② as a woman, she would not be able to lead a 12-mile hike >!

   < ① Madelyn could not be a leader of her son's scouting troop >
   < ② No woman would be able to lead a 12-mile hike >
   [< ③ All leaders of their son's scouting troops must be able to lead a 12-mile hike >]
   [< ④ Madelyn is a woman >]

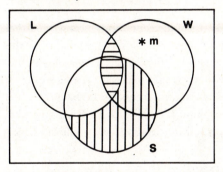

KEY
m abbreviates Madelyn
L abbreviates the class of things that
   can lead a 12-mile hike
W abbreviates the class of women
S abbreviates the class of things that
   can lead their son's scouting troops

12-17   He < ① [Sartre] did not write like a philosopher > either, (for) < ② he commanded
a graceful prose style >.

   < ② Sartre commanded a graceful prose style >
   [< ③ No philosopher commands a graceful prose style >]

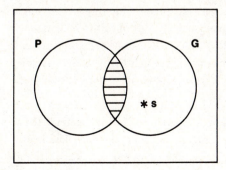

KEY
s abbreviates Sartre
P abbreviates the class of things that
   write like philosophers
G abbreviates the class of things that
   command a graceful prose style

12-19 < ① André must use a pencil to dial a telephone >, (because) < ② his fingers won't fit the holes in the dial >

< ③ André's fingers won't fit the holes in the dial of a telephone >
[< ④ Anything whose fingers won't fit the holes in the dial of a telephone must use a pencil to dial a telephone >]

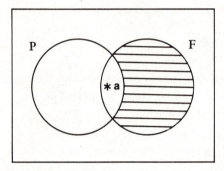

KEY
a abbreviates André
P abbreviates the class of things that must use a pencil to dial a telephone
F abbreviates the class of things whose fingers won't fit the holes in the dial of a telephone

Section 13

13-3 This is a paradigm argument from authority. Clinique comes to the conclusion that soap is best for cleaning faces on the evidence that dermatologists (generally) say this and that dermatologists are appropriate authorities on the subject. Dermatologists are, of course, the relevant authorities on matters such as this, so this is a strong argument from authority. Note that this is a strong argument for the conclusion that *soap* is best for cleaning faces; it is, however, not any reason for favoring Clinique over any other soap. (To draw the conclusion that Clinique is best for cleaning faces would be to commit the straw man fallacy—see Section 15.)

13-11 This is a humorous use of the slippery slope argument. However, although we are not supposed to take the conclusion seriously, the use of the slippery slope argument here well displays what is often wrong when this argument is used seriously. There clearly is a progression that we can imagine from chopsticks, through forks, tablespoons, soup ladles, to dory-bailers. Also, if the evidence of his books is to be believed, we can easily imagine Calvin Trillin and his cohorts eating with tablespoons. But though they might get that far along in this "escalating instruments race," it is difficult to imagine their getting any further. (Would eating with a dory-bailer increase one's "stuffing power"? It certainly would be a lot messier.) Thus no one would be likely to slip all the way down the slope, even if they started out on it. This is typical in the case of slippery slope arguments.

13-21 This is a case of the fallacy of irrelevant reason. Margaret explains the reason (itself an argument from authority) for believing that there is a time for everything. This is absolutely no reason at all for believing that the sign of the moon indicates when a thing's time has come—and this is the issue Margaret is supposed to be addressing—so this "argument" has no worth at all. (This might be considered to be a very poor straw man argument—poor, because the conclusion Margaret in fact argues for and the one she should be arguing for are so different. For the straw man argument, see Section 15.)

13–26 The evidence that Falwell cites is that Jesus Christ did not speak up against capital punishment on an occasion on which he could have. Falwell draws the conclusion from this that Jesus Christ was not against capital punishment. This is clearly an argument from ignorance. Should we conclude that Jesus Christ was not against, for example, prostitution because he did not use the cross as a platform to denounce it? Moreover, it is easy to imagine why Jesus Christ might not, on the cross, have spoken up against capital punishment even if he was against it—perhaps, for example, he would not have wanted people to think that he was just trying to save his own skin.

Notice that after having thus argued for the conclusion that Jesus Christ was in favor of capital punishment, Falwell then uses this conclusion in a further argument. The further argument is, once again, an argument from authority. Falwell clearly concludes that capital punishment is acceptable on the basis that Jesus Christ thought it acceptable. Given what Falwell believes about Jesus Christ, that would, of course, be a fairly good argument from authority.

Section 14

14–8 This is a classic case of the questionable cause fallacy. Pare argues from the fact that a decline in baptism has been accompanied by a (supposed) rise in demonic activity to the conclusion that baptism is (at least, partially) causally responsible for a low level of demonic activity. Even if we are prepared to concede that there is such a thing as demonic activity, and even if there is this correlation, there is no evidence for the causal conclusion. We could just as well argue that the increased demonic activity caused fewer people to get baptized. And, where the evidence is equally good for both of these conflicting causal claims, there is no real evidence for either. (This is often the situation when the fallacy of questionable cause is committed.) This is thus a bad argument.

Note that the first paragraph contains an argument from authority. We are invited to accept the claim that possession occurs in one person in 500 on the basis that this claim has been made by a "respected senior cleric of Church of England."

Also note that although it is probably unintentional, there are the makings of a reasonably strong ad hominem argument in this piece. Pare claims that demonic activity is up, and Pare is an "exorcist for the Oxford diocese"—that is, someone whose job depends on people believing that there is demonic activity to be dealt with. Clearly, he is an interested party. In such cases, we have some grounds for suspicion as to the accuracy of the remarks of the interested party. Of course, if we think that clerics are no more capable of distorting the truth than they are of chopping down cherry trees, we will feel the ad hominem is, in this case, undermined.

14-11 This example is typical of the way in which fallacies often occur in advertisements—they are *all but* committed. Clearly, the ad wants us to think that part of the "feeling better" comes from having put Oil of Olay on our face—though they don't actually state this. To so conclude would, of course, be to commit the fallacy of questionable cause—the "feeling better" almost certainly comes from stopping studying for 15 minutes to listen to some quiet music and "stretch like a lazy cat." So although the ad tempts us to commit the fallacy, the text of the ad does not itself actually commit the fallacy. The argument to the implicit conclusion would, of course, be a bad argument. Strictly speaking, as it is, there is no argument in the ad—good or bad.

14-31 This is an argument from analogy. There are, of course, features in common between getting married and getting a new dog—both involve a shakedown period while you get to know each other's habits and territory. However, there are important differences. In a marriage the woman selects the man to the same extent that the man selects the woman. But dogs don't select their owners (don't kid yourself—those puppies lick everyone's hand). We usually know a little more about the person we marry before getting married than we typically know about the dog we acquire. Yard work is working out how to make the dog do what you want it to do. Marriage, even for the most autocratic of humans, typically involves more give and take than that. Of course, there is a male chauvinist rhetoric that denies these differences (and this, presumably, is why the item appeared in *New Woman*), but that rhetoric has never very accurately described the marriage situation. The differences (*dis*analogies) are so great here, compared with the similarities (analogies) between the two cases, that this is definitely a questionable analogy. Any conclusion based on the analogy would be suspect. Thus this is a bad argument.

14-33 In this argument various charges are made about Sidote, and various facts about his past are brought up in an attempt to undermine his claims. This is all summed up when the author says that Sidote's past "casts a shadow over his veracity." Because one of the charges is that Sidote is a liar, this has the makings of a good argument in the context of the courtroom. Assuming that it is established that Sidote is a liar, there is then no reason to believe his claims against Foat. As there was, in this case, little other evidence against Foat, no charge against her is established, and so she must be acquitted. Note that the fact that Sidote is a liar does not establish that he is lying in this case (liars sometimes tell the truth, of necessity, to maintain their credibility). Thus the fact that Sidote is a liar does not establish that Foat is innocent—but for Foat to be acquitted, that does not have to be established. We are not trying to suggest that Foat *is* guilty. The point is that the most that is established even by a good ad hominem argument is that we have no reason to believe the original claims made by the subject who is now under attack. Such an argument does not give us reason to think that these claims are false.

Section 15

15-1 This is the fallacy of inconsistency. Making this statement halfway through ten songs constitutes interrupting those songs. Thus making the statement is inconsistent with what the statement claims. Presumably, this is only an inconsistency strictly speaking. No doubt what was intended by the statement was that the ten songs would be played without any intervening commercials. That, of course, is consistent with making the statement in the passage.

15-12 This is an excellent example of red herring. Bailes is supposed to be apologizing to Denton, but a careful reading of his statement shows that he does no such thing. Instead, he waffles for a while and then sidetracks to jingoistic remarks about Alabama patriots.

What makes the passage amusing is that Denton doesn't seem to notice. The apology isn't incomplete—it's not there at all.

15-15 Here is another example of how fallacies occur in advertising material. By being told that one pound of shrimp meat is enough protein for six people, we are being invited to draw the conclusion that a pound of shrimp meat would serve six people. But if we are concerned to get our daily minimum protein requirement, we probably won't be eating shrimp. So in serving sizes the amount of protein is essentially irrelevant. What matters is what it looks like on the plate. Try serving a sixth of a pound of shrimp.

Of course, the ad doesn't actually say that a pound of shrimp will feed six. But the advertisers know that, when it comes to shrimp, protein requirements aren't the most important consideration. It is difficult to see the relevance of this claim unless it is an attempt to get us to draw this related, but importantly different, conclusion. It seems fair to conclude that the passage implicitly contains an example of the straw man fallacy.

15-21 This illustrates the fallacy of circularity. The reason given for saying that natural food additives are declining proportionately is that synthetic additives are increasing proportionately. But there are only natural and synthetic additives—so if one declines proportionately, the other must increase. The "reason" and the "conclusion" say the same thing. There is no real argument here at all.

Section 16

16-8 The Shriners may know exactly how many operations had been performed, but if they do, in fact, only know the number approximately, the figure should not be given as it is: '349,492' belies what is conveyed by 'approximately'. If the figure is only known to the nearest ten or hundred then it should be stated as 349,490 or 349,500 respectively, to give the reader some idea of the degree of accuracy of the figure. Similar comments apply to the number of x-rays and photos taken.

Finally, it seems strange that they know the exact numbers for braces and prostheses, for physical therapy treatment, and for clinic visits, but only approximate numbers for operations. There is reason to be suspicious of the accuracy of all these claims. (It could be the case, however, that some records were destroyed whereas others were not. Such a fact could explain away the suspicion—but the suspicion remains until it is explained away.)

16-9 A study of 51 children does not seem very large, so we might suspect the fallacy of small sample.

What is most surprising, however, is the causal conclusion in the second paragraph. The doctors observe that more battered infants are low in weight at birth; thus they speculate that low birthweight might be a (partial) cause of child beating. A different causal story seems more plausible. Children who are going to be beaten by their parents are probably born to less caring parents. Less caring parents are more likely to have neglected the prenatal care of the child. Neglecting the prenatal care of the child is likely to lead to low birthweight. Thus being the kind of person who is more inclined to beat a child probably causes the child to be born underweight. This seems a more likely explanation than that adults are more likely to beat a puny child.

As all the doctors have to go on is the correlation, and as an equally (or more) plausible cause can be made for a different causal claim, their argument from the correlation to the causal claim is weak.

16-12 "Ten percent," in the statement that Alabama has 10 percent of the nation's natural resources, is a suspiciously round figure. Also, what counts as a natural resource? Coal, oil, iron ore, and limestone? Labor? Hydropower and available solar energy? The lack of clear meaning to 'natural resource' and the roundness of 10 percent suggest that this is at best a "guesstimate."

Similar comments apply to "support for law enforcement." Is this just the amount of money devoted to police departments? Or does it attempt to include such intangibles as how supportive Alabamians are of their police?

Most interesting is the switch from the ranking of Alabama in the 50 states to her ranking in the 14 southern states. Presumably, the worst-looking statistics were chosen. For all we can tell from the last four statistical claims, Alabama might have been twelfth, thirteenth, and fourteenth out of the 50 states. Although the picture is probably not that distorted, these figures cover the end of the period of growth in the "sunbelt." In these categories Alabama was probably well above last in the 50 states.

Even taking the statistics at their face value, they don't support the conclusion that Alabama is always last (which is implicit in "I'm tired of Alabama always being last")—and when looked at critically, there is probably no case where Alabama is last.

This is a very bad argument—but a very good example of the manipulation of statistics by a politician.

16–19 The votes of 24 people out of the whole of the U.S. voting population are too small to draw any conclusion—a fallacy of small sample.

The sample comes from Dixville, New Hampshire, a town with 24 registered voters—obviously a very small town. Small towns are more conservative than the American population at large. New Hampshire is probably more conservative than the nation at large. A small town in New Hampshire is almost certain to be more conservative than the general U.S. population. So the sample is not only too small, it is also biased.

The fact that this community has "predicted" two presidential elections in the last 20 years is interesting. Depending on how we count, the 20 years could include the previous four or five presidential elections. So Dixville "got the answer right" no better than 50 percent of the time (and perhaps worse than that). Thinking about recent American presidential elections, this probably means that they "predicted" the two times when Nixon was elected. Thus their voting record is probably compatible with their voting conservatively no matter what the rest of the country is doing. This is somewhat confirmed by noting that in the 1980 election—the subject of this passage—Dixville voted proportionately more conservatively than the country at large. If they consistently vote conservatively, they are hardly a weathervane for the political climate of the country. (Rather, they are more like the clock that is "right" twice every 24 hours because it is stopped.)

From this evidence we clearly can't draw any sensible conclusion about the outcome of the election. (This is true even though, as we now know, they once again "got the answer right.") It should be said in defense of WBHM that this item was almost certainly included in the newscast for its amusement value.